D0688841

WASHINGTON
THEN & NOW

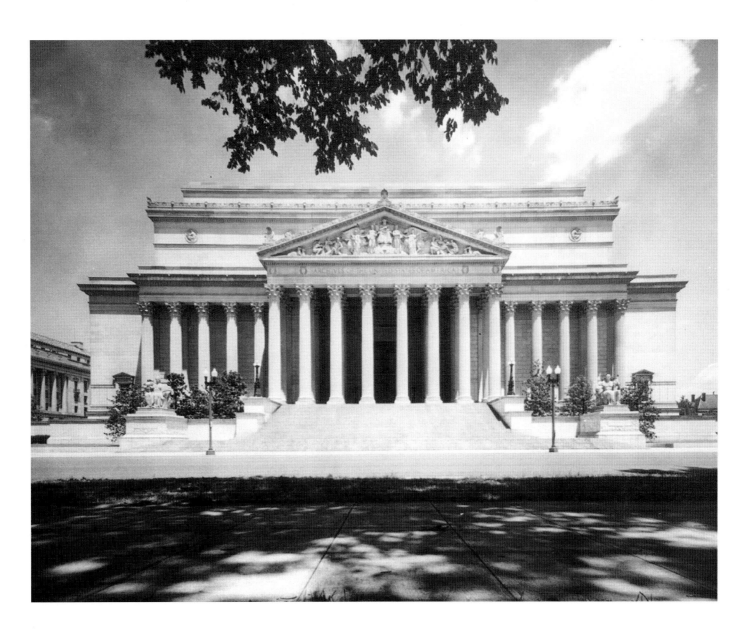

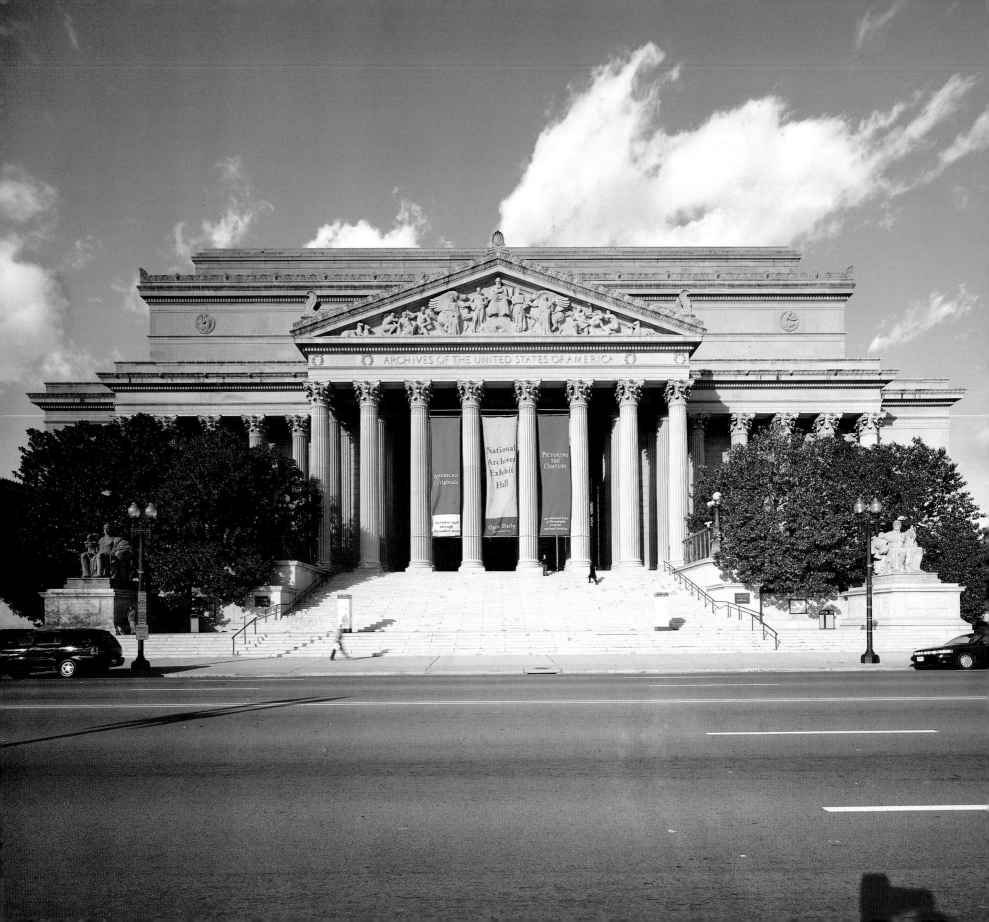

WASHINGTON THEN & NOW

ALEXANDER D. MITCHELL IV

THUNDER BAY
P·R·E·S·S

Published in the United States by
Thunder Bay Press
An imprint of the Advantage Publishers Group
5880 Oberlin Drive
San Diego, CA 92121-4794
www.advantagebooksonline.com

All notations of errors or omissions should be
addressed to Thunder Bay Press, editorial department,
at the above address. All other correspondence (author
inquiries, permissions and rights) concerning the
content of this book should be addressed to PRC
Publishing Ltd, Kiln House, 210 New Kings Road,
London SW6 4NZ

ISBN 1-57145-191-9

Library of Congress Cataloging-in-Publication data
available upon request.

Printed and bound in China.

1 2 3 4 5 00 01 02 03 04

Right: One of only two significant floods
to strike downtown Washington (the other
the result of a February 1881 ice jam), the
June 1889 flood also did significant
damage to other parts of the Middle
Atlantic States as well. In the case of
Washington, the primary flooding was due
to inadequate drainage, and affected
principally this area of Pennsylvania
Avenue, which lies in what had been Tiber
Creek before the development of the
District.

Pages One & Two: The National Archives
(see pages 90–91).

ACKNOWLEDGMENTS

The publisher wishes to thank Simon Clay for taking all the color photographs for this book. The back cover photograph was supplied courtesy of
© James Marshall/CORBIS. The photograph on page 139 was supplied courtesy of © CORBIS. The black and white photography was supplied courtesy of the
Prints and Photographs Division of the Library of Congress, with the following exceptions:
© CORBIS for the front cover;
Daguerreotype Collection, Prints and Photographs Division, Library of Congress for page 6;
© S. W. Gerber, Prints and Photographs Division, Library of Congress for page 8 (right);
Theodor Horydczak Collection, Prints and Photographs Division, Library of Congress for page 20;
Historical Society of Washington, D.C. for page 24;
Selected Civil War Photographs, 1861–1865 Collection, Prints and Photographs Division, Library of Congress for page 26 (inset);
Historic American Buildings Survey Collection, Prints and Photographs Division, Library of Congress for pages 68 and 114;
© Detroit Photo Co., Prints and Photographs Division, Library of Congress for page 88 (main);
© American Press Association, Prints and Photographs Division, Library of Congress for page 108;
James M. Goode Collection, Prints and Photographs Division, Library of Congress for page 110;
© Bettmann/CORBIS for page 138;
Hulton Getty Picture Collection for page 140.

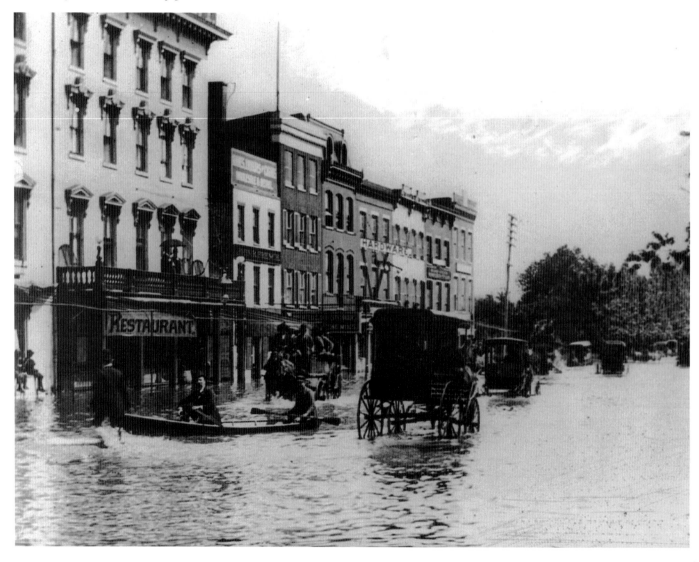

INTRODUCTION

O f all the major cities in the United States, Washington, D.C., must rate as the most untypical and unusual. It is often regarded as the center of power of the United States, and even Western civilization. It could qualify as the first "planned community" in the U.S., even if the plans were often disregarded and changed over the years. It merits nomination as the largest "company town," what with the huge numbers of federal employees now working in the city. The city's skyline is distinguished by what it doesn't have—an abundance of skyscrapers rising out of the downtown district. And the District of Columbia is truly "monumental," with a memorial, monument, or grand building seemingly within sight or a stone's throw of any place in town.

The area now known as the District of Columbia had its origins in 1785 when, after years of a nomadic existence, the new government of the 13 former British colonies voted to set up shop in a permanent "federal town." After much debate over whether to place the city on the Delaware River or the Potomac River, the government decided on the southern option. In 1790 George Washington himself selected the 100-square-mile diamond of land that would be named after him. It incorporated parts of Alexandria, Virginia (near his own home at Mount Vernon), Georgetown, Maryland, and both banks of the Potomac and Anacostia rivers. The location would be derided in future years as a location heavy on swamps and mosquitoes, hot and humid in the summer and cold and icy in the winter.

Pierre Charles L'Enfant, a French engineer and architect who had served with Washington in the Colonial army, offered his services to design a capital city worthy of a great nation and world recognition. No doubt inspired by the grandeur of Versailles and Paris, he and Andrew Ellicott laid out a visionary grid plan heavy with majestic avenues, a central mall, monumental circles, and spectacular public buildings—the basis of Washington's heart today.

L'Enfant's plan quickly outran the young nation's resources and the ability of economic development to match, and it would take until the era after the Civil War for the combination of a thriving economy and expanding government to raise the city from a backwater company town to a metropolis. By 1900, however, unplanned and haphazard development had so ignored the L'Enfant plan's vision that a congressional committee headed by Senator James McMillan was organized to completely revamp and overhaul the future appearance of Washington. The end result of consultations with architects and artists was the Senate Park Commission Report for Washington, popularly referred to as the McMillan Plan, released in 1902, which would affect the appearance of the city for decades, if not forever. Its major effects over the years were to restore and protect the open spaces of the Mall and create other open plazas and monuments such as the Union Station Plaza, the Lincoln Memorial, and the Arlington Memorial Bridge. It also capped the height of future buildings just as the skyscraper era began, producing the low-slung skyline that distinguishes the city today from almost every other American metropolitan area.

The next major plan for Washington arose from the Public Buildings Commission, created by Congress in 1916 to address the problems of housing an expanding bureaucracy. Their planning culminated in the Public Buildings Act of 1928, which directly resulted in the construction during the Depression-ridden 1930s of the group of massive federal buildings between Pennsylvania Avenue and the Mall now known as Federal Triangle. It also resulted in the construction of the Supreme Court Building, the House Office Building, and the Jefferson Memorial.

In common with metropolitan areas in the rest of the nation after World War II, Washington shifted from a thriving residential metropolis to a central business city surrounded by suburban bedroom communities. In all this the downtown shopping district and much of Pennsylvania Avenue, arguably the nation's showcase boulevard, remained neglected. In 1964 a President's Council on Pennsylvania Avenue, appointed by the late President John F. Kennedy, submitted a report that guided the redesign of the southeastern end of Pennsylvania Avenue and the commercial district to the north between 6th and 9th streets. The redevelopment continues to this day.

Today, Washington continues as a thriving American city, although not without the ills affecting every other American city—crime, suburbanization, traffic congestion, etc.—and troubles unique to the District of Columbia (political wrangling, Watergate, etc.). As the 21st Century approached, the District itself struggled to get aboard the economic boom that had swept the post-Cold War United States, and struggled anew to gain political autonomy in the form of home rule or statehood.

This book, just like the photographs inside, cannot be a definitive interpretation or history of a city. Rather, it is a moment frozen in time, sometimes perilously. For every scene in the book that is seemingly preserved for the ages by planning and legislation, there is another where construction cranes hover and buildings are rising or falling as these words are written. For every scene that would take no effort for the first-time visitor to find, there were scenes that led to enormous perplexity and searching. Jonathan Swift noted that "there is nothing in this world constant, but inconstancy," and that is particularly apt in the case of photographic histories. With that, I hope that you enjoy the small slice of the District of Columbia's historic panorama I was able to bring you, and hope that readers in the future can also partake in the sense of discovery and exploration that we enjoyed while producing this book.

Alexander D. Mitchell IV

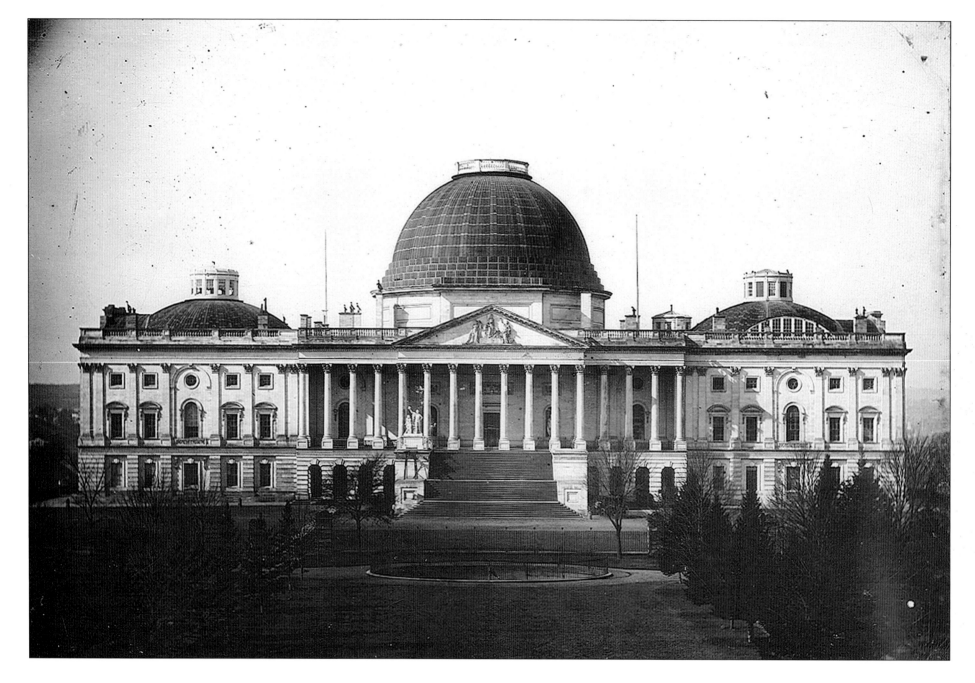

The earliest known photograph of the Capitol, this 1846 daguerreotype is one of a series taken of Washington subjects by John Plumbe, Jr., regarded by many as the first professional photographer in the country. Seven are known to survive, including this one, among a set purchased at a flea market in Alameda, California, in 1971 for only a few dollars and subsequently sold to the Library of Congress. The old Senate wing, begun in 1793 and completed in 1800, is to the right; the House wing is to the left. Both were torched by British troops in August 1814 during the War of 1812.

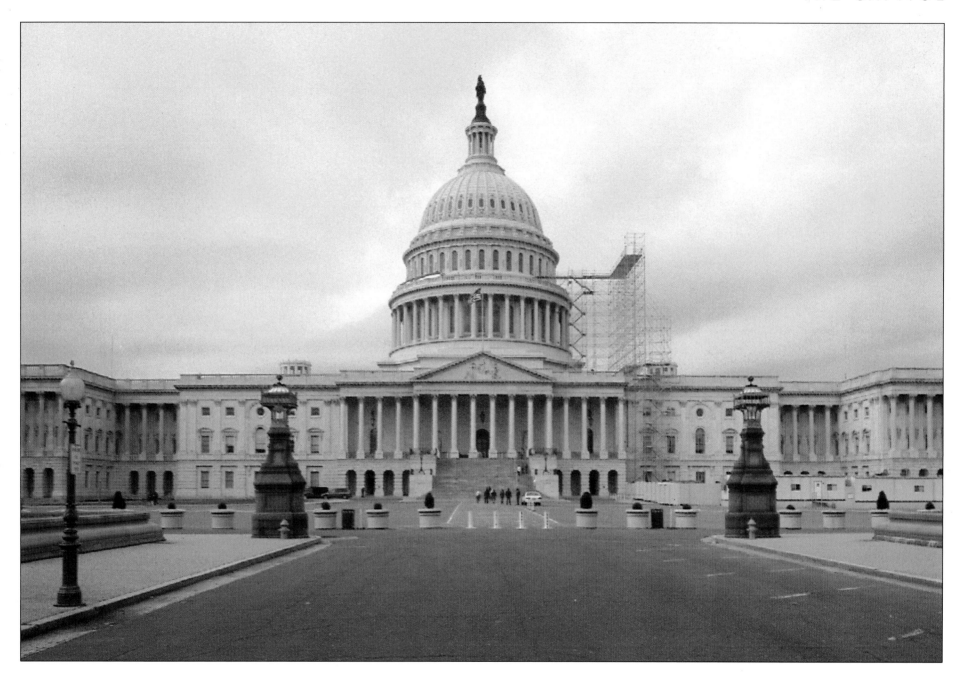

After rebuilding the fire-devastated wings, Charles Bulfinch began work on the center section in 1818, completing it in 1829. The masonry inner dome was shrouded with the wood-and-copper dome depicted. The scaffolding shown is construction access to an ongoing renovation of the newer iron dome.

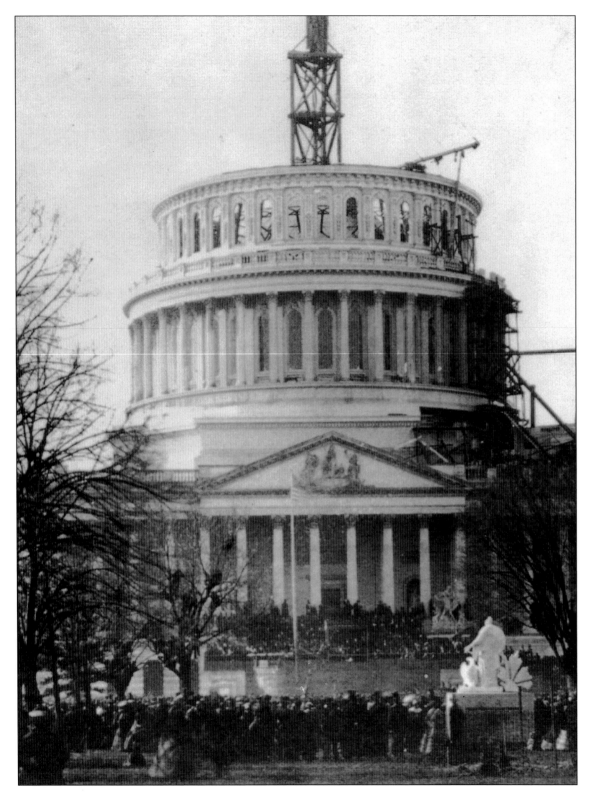

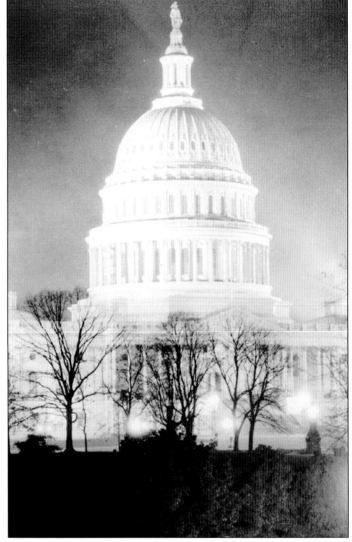

In 1850, Congress (which had grown along with the nation) authorized a badly needed expansion of the Capitol, begun the following year. Subsequently, in 1855 Congress authorized a larger dome in keeping with the larger building. The photo on the left depicts the March 4, 1861, inauguration ceremony of Abraham Lincoln, while the dome was still under construction.

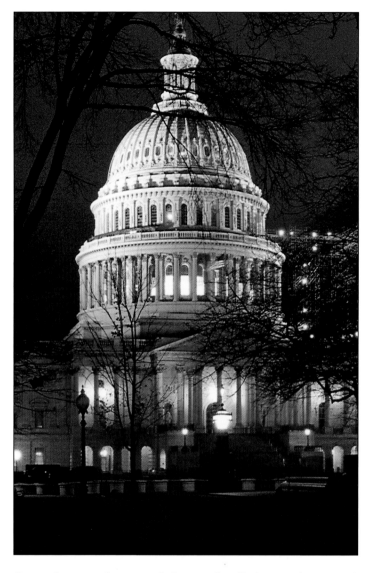

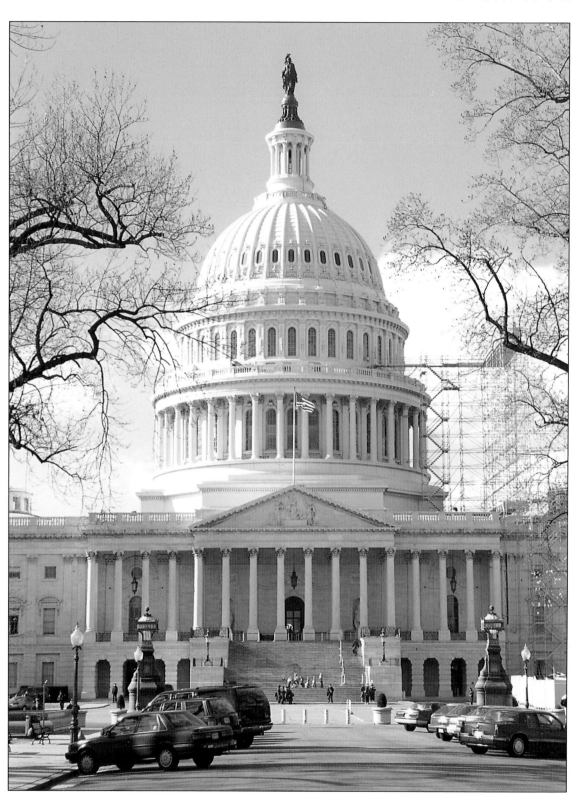

Since the introduction of electric floodlighting, the seat of national government has been bathed in a spectacular blaze of glory nightly, save for wartime blackouts. The modern photo shows what appears to be the same portico and walls, but actually shows a new extension built 34 feet out from the old one in 1959–61, which added 100 additional offices.

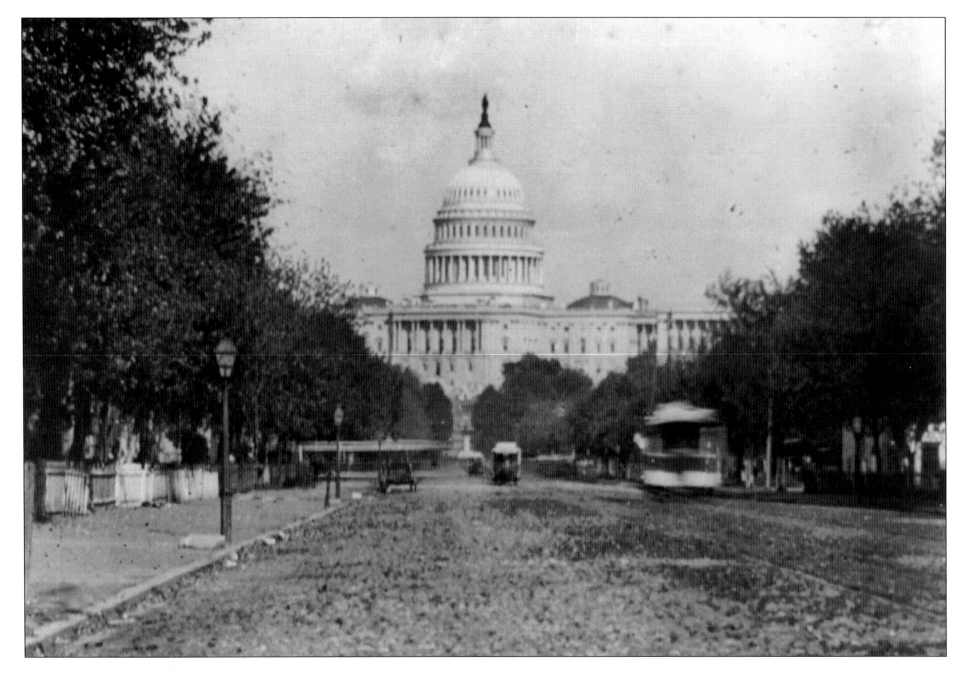

Looking northeast on Maryland Avenue, this view from around 1891 shows the Capitol as completed, as well as three blurred horse-drawn streetcars. Horse-drawn streetcars began operation in Washington in 1862. The first electric streetcars in the city began operation in 1880, but overhead wires were banned by Congress very quickly afterward. It took several years for an effective underground conduit system to be developed, a system which gave the trackage the appearance of a cable car system like San Francisco's.

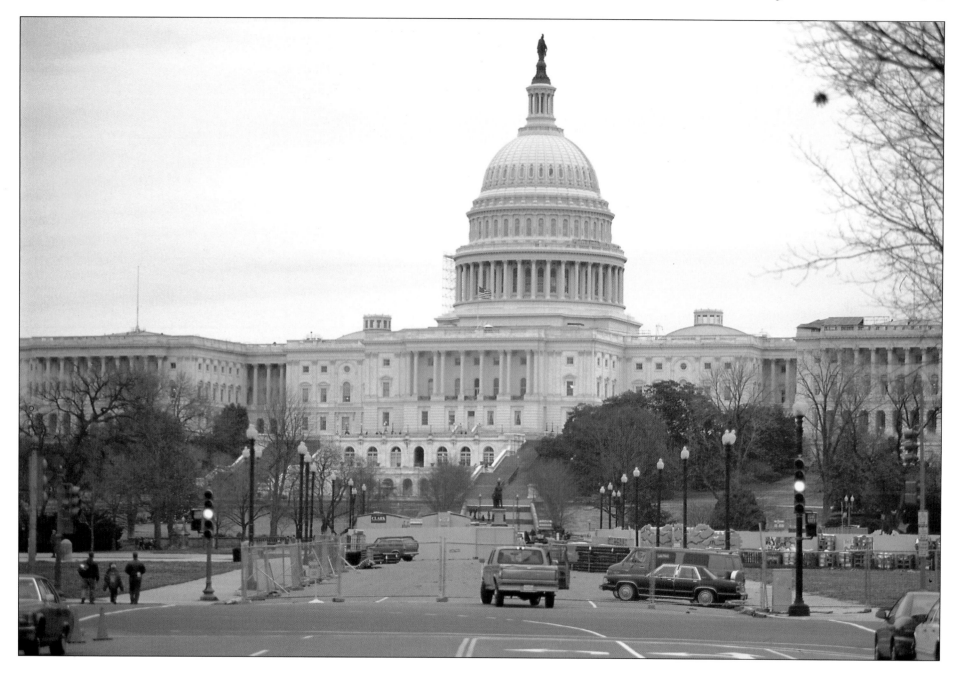

The last D.C. Transit streetcars operated in January 1962; the Washington Metro subway system was begun in 1969 and opened in 1976. The modern view shows little has changed, other than a change in streetlight hardware and a reduction in foliage. The 19-foot bronze statue atop the Capitol dome, *Freedom*, sculpted by Thomas Crawford, was removed from its perch by helicopter for a much-needed cleaning in 1993.

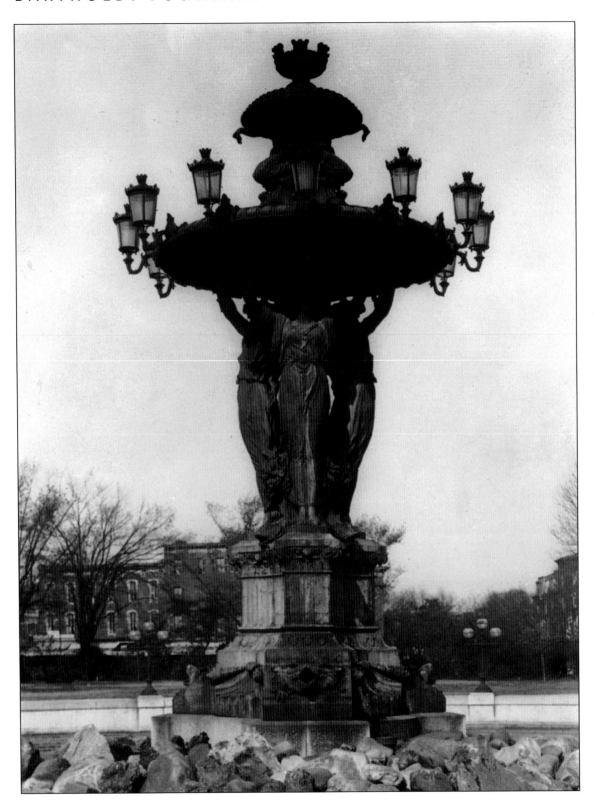

French sculptor Frédéric Auguste Bartholdi produced many of the world's most renowned sculptures including, arguably the most famous of all, "Liberty Enlightening the World," known more popularly as the Statue of Liberty in New York Harbor. This fountain, humble by comparison, was built for the Centennial Exhibition in Philadelphia in 1876 and was purchased by the government in 1877.

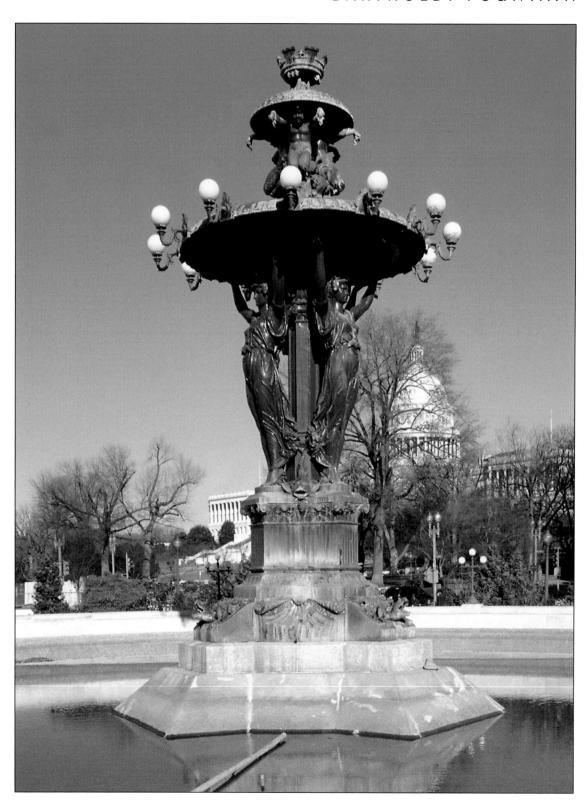

Originally installed in the Botanic Garden across the street from the Capitol, the Bartholdi Fountain was moved in 1932 to a small triangle west of the Rayburn Senate Building and above Washington Avenue, which is now effectively the end of a major exit ramp from the Southwest/Southeast Freeway (I-395). Thousands of drivers struggle past this fountain daily, perhaps never knowing its significance.

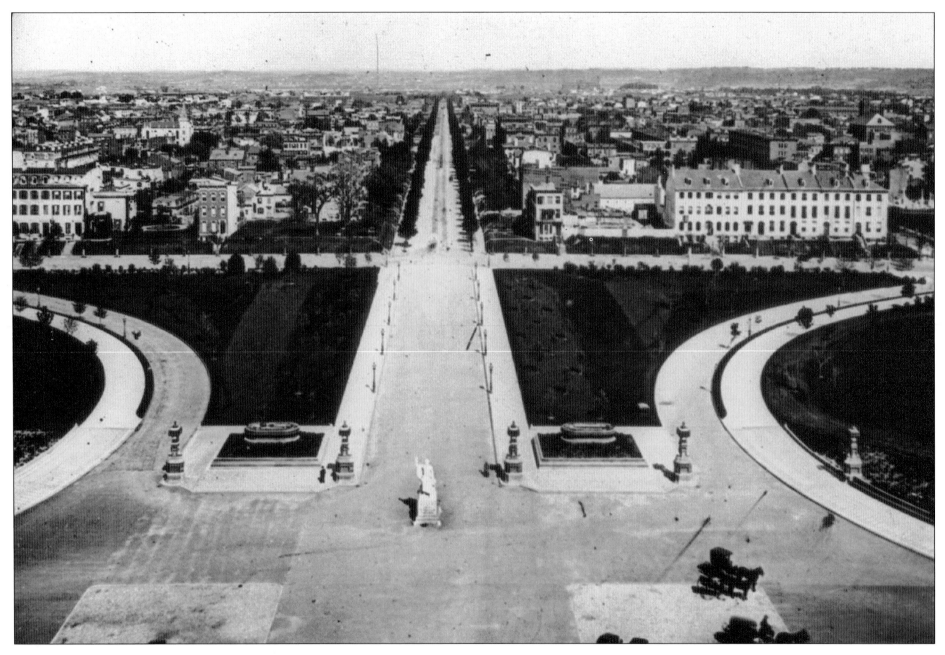

The view east from the Capitol dome in about 1880 depicts the largely-residential neighborhood now referred to as Capitol Hill. The massive (20-ton) marble statue of George Washington in the foreground, done by Horatio Greenough, was commissioned by Congress in 1832 and delivered in 1841. It proved to be too heavy for the Rotunda yet oddly too small for the interior, and it spent the next century being moved about the East Grounds and the city like a hapless chess pawn before taking up residence in the Smithsonian's

Museum of History & Technology in 1962. At the right center can be seen Carroll Row, the future site of the Library of Congress. Large numbers of newer Victorian homes can also be seen, as can the results of general public works and street regrading—many older buildings are now high above the streets, requiring long stair climbs to the front door.

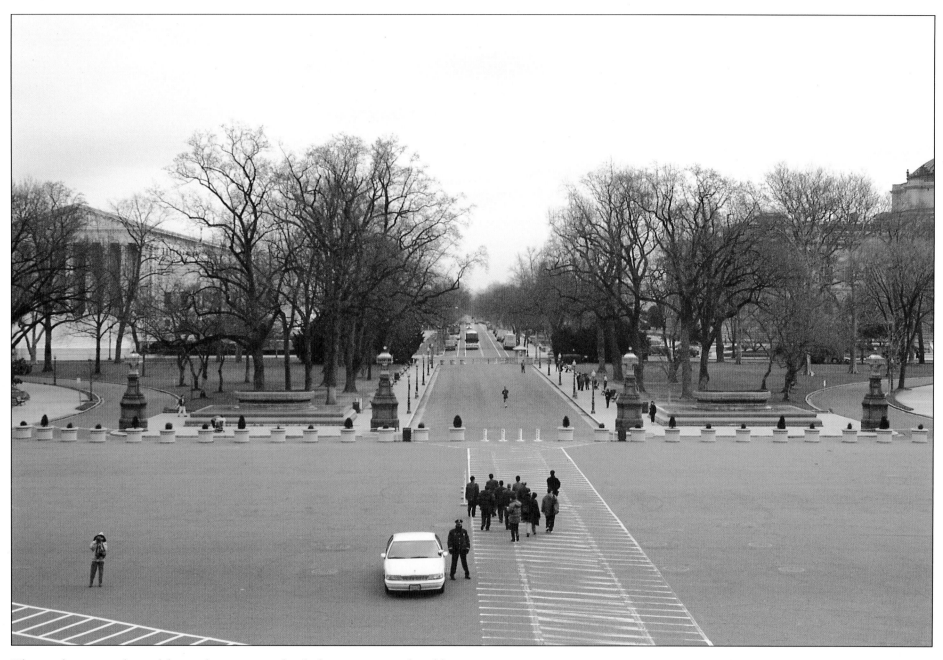

The modern view shows foliage obscuring much of what appears in the old photograph, but to the left can be seen the Supreme Court Building and to the right, beyond the trees, the Library of Congress. Note also the concessions to modern security—a heavy police presence and "decorative" planters that actually serve as barricades. Tripods, a necessity in early photography, are not even permitted on the Capitol grounds without permits.

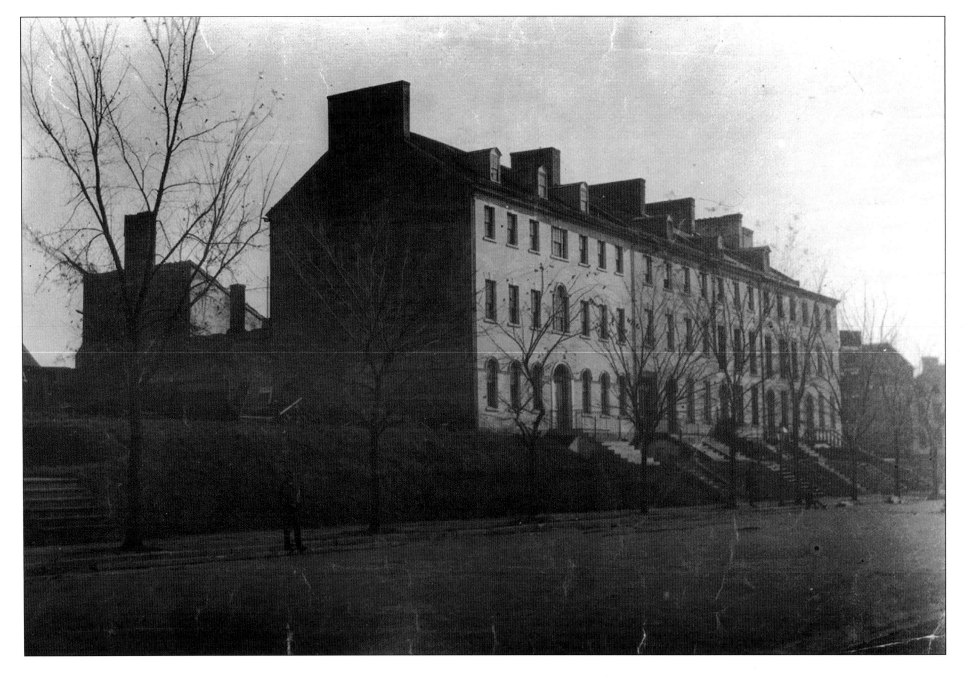

Built in 1805 by Daniel Carroll, this row of houses, literally across the street from the Capitol grounds, was leased to local innkeeper Pontius D. Stelle, who rented rooms to the earliest members of Congress and their visitors and business associates. It was also, oddly, used to house political prisoners during the Civil War.

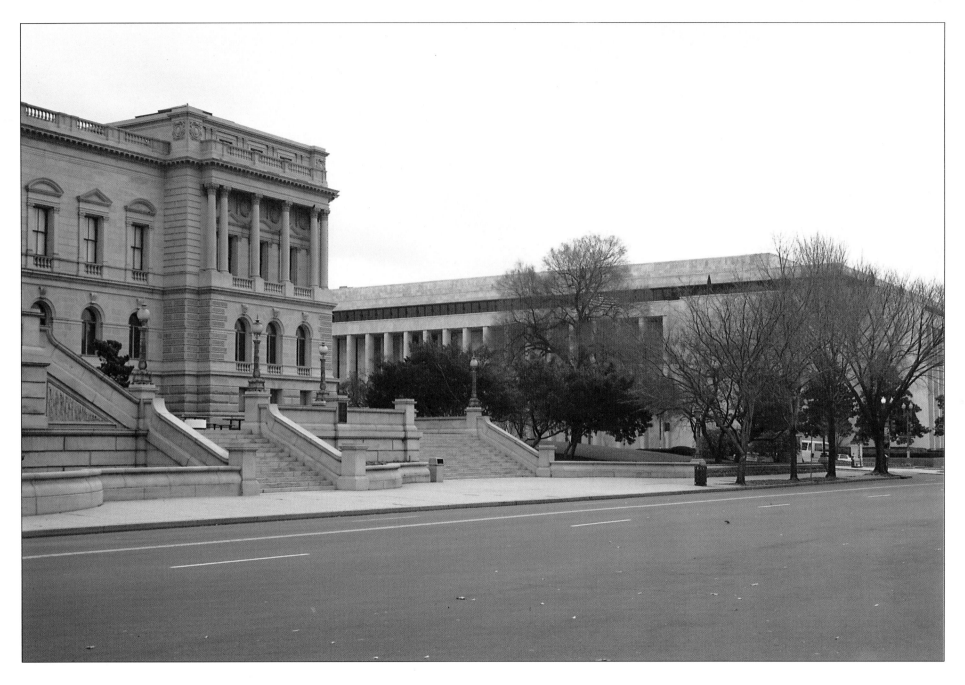

The row of houses was demolished in 1886–87 to make way for the Jefferson Building of the Library of Congress, seen to the left of the modern photograph. Behind and to the south of the Jefferson Building across Independence Avenue is the newer Madison Building of the Library of Congress, opened in 1980.

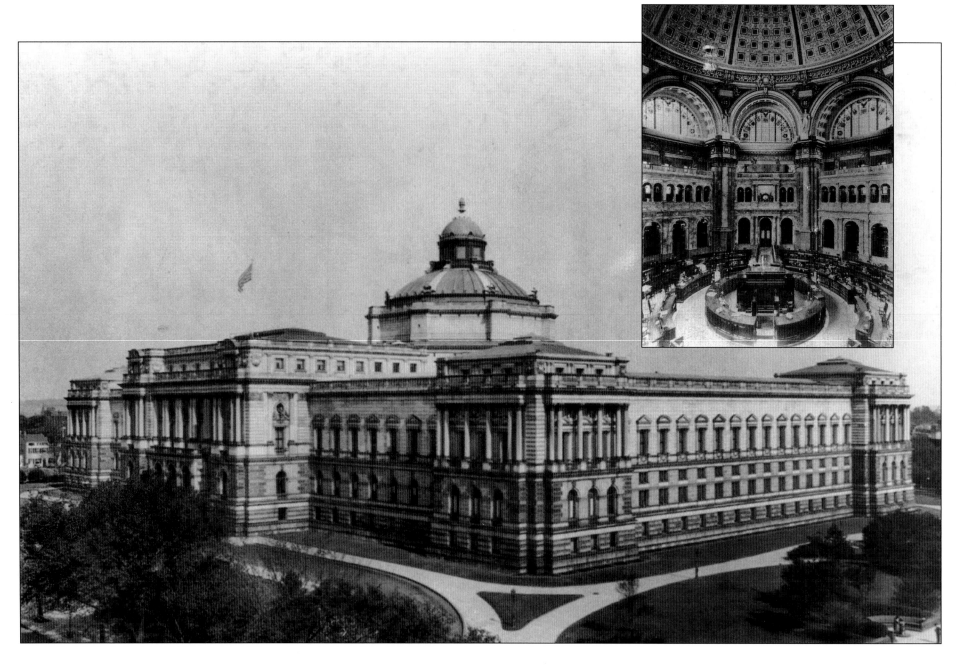

The Library of Congress was started as a legislative library in 1800 with the acquisition of 740 books from London, but was destroyed when the British burned Washington in 1814. Thomas Jefferson then sold his 6,437-volume personal library to the government for $23,950 to form the nucleus for a new library. Since then, the Library of Congress has become the de facto national library of virtually all published works in the United States. A more modern library building, now known as the Jefferson Building, was planned in 1871, with construction begun in 1886 and completion in 1897. This photograph was taken in 1921.

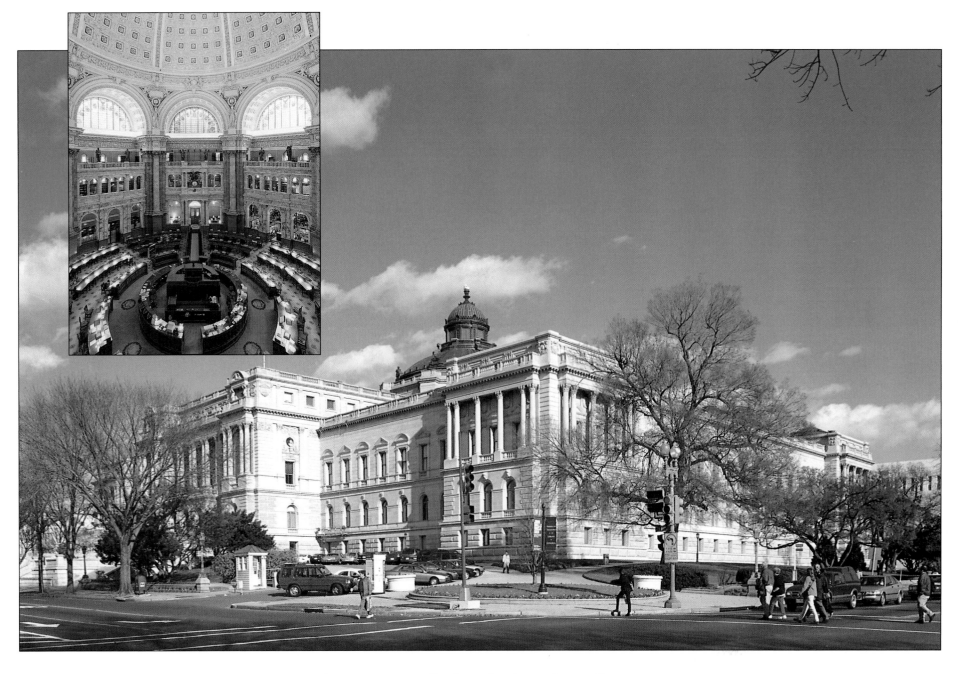

The Jefferson Building, built to Italian Renaissance design, was originally planned to house three million volumes; the Library of Congress at the time of writing houses over 100 million items and employs nearly 5,000 people over three adjoining buildings (Jefferson, Adams, and Madison) and offsite storage. The inset photos show the Main Reading Room, an awe-inspiring room described as being like the interior of a giant Fabergé egg. Only the glow of laptop computers in half of the room marks the difference of years in the octagonal mahogany-trimmed shrine to research.

THE GREAT HALL, LIBRARY OF CONGRESS

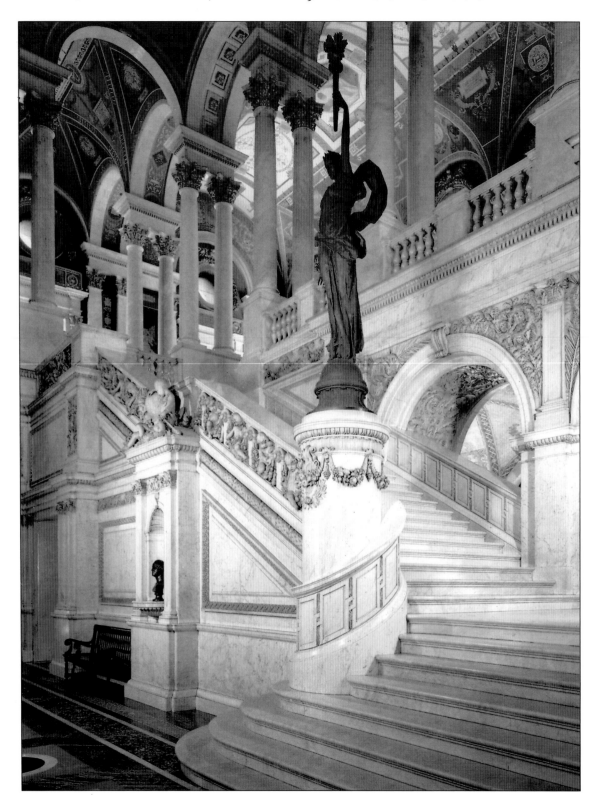

The gem of the Jefferson Building of the Library of Congress, and arguably the whole of Washington, is its spectacular, richly decorated Great Hall. In spite of the outlandish decoration of the building, the building was originally completed for $200,000 less than the original Congressional authorization of $6,500,000. Of that, the costs of painting, sculpture, decoration, and three massive bronze doors was $364,000.

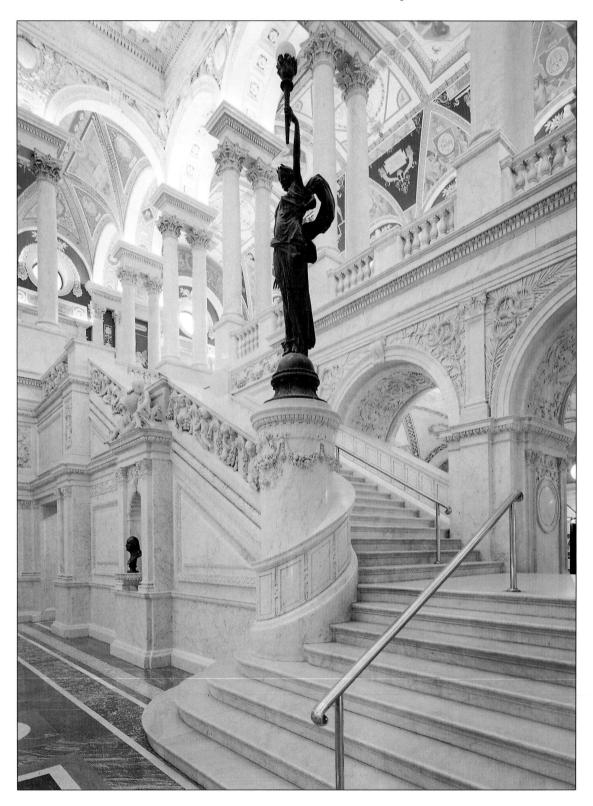

After eleven years of renovation of its curving marble staircases, bronze statuary, rich mosaics, and paintings and murals that would be the envy of ancient Egypt or Greece, the Jefferson Building was reopened to the public in 1997, the building's centennial year, and today it is as impressive as it was when it was opened—a superb and painstaking job of restoration.

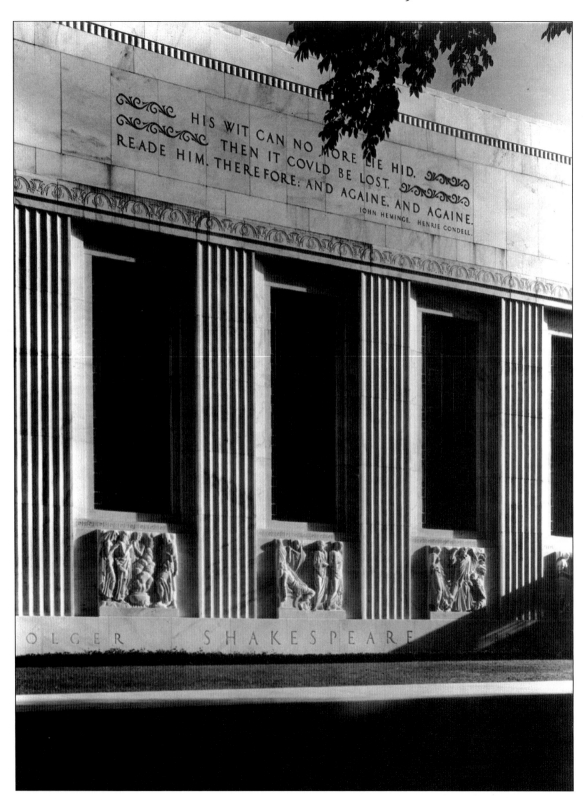

Opened in 1932 and located just down Capitol Street from the Library of Congress (but an independent concern), the Folger Shakespeare Library was a gift to the American people from Henry Clay Folger and his wife Emily Jordan Folger. The marble Art Deco building was designed by architect Paul Philippe Cret.

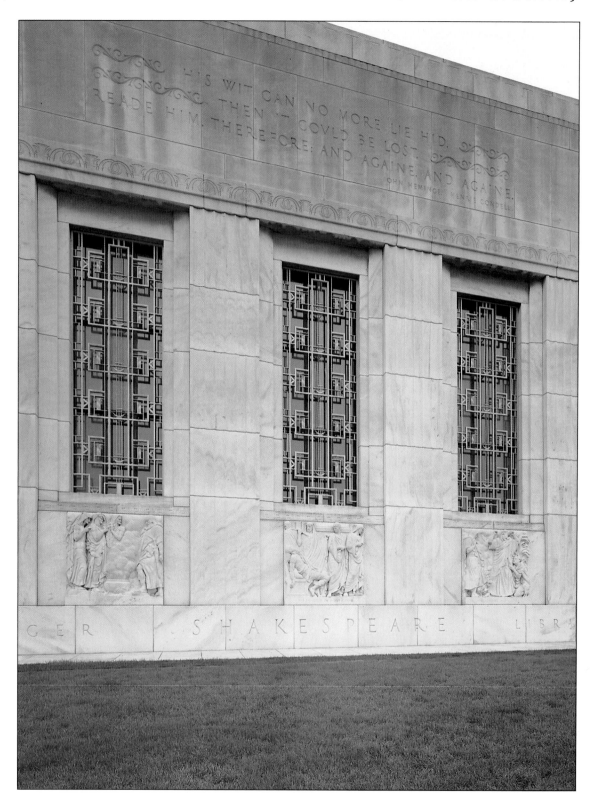

A major center for research, the Folger houses the world's largest collection of Shakespeare's printed works, in addition to a large collection of other rare Renaissance books and manuscripts on disciplines such as history, theology, politics, and the arts. The collection consists of approximately 280,000 books and manuscripts; 27,000 paintings, drawings, engravings, and prints; and musical instruments, costumes, and films. Also inside is a reproduction inn-yard theater, used for theatrical and musical performances.

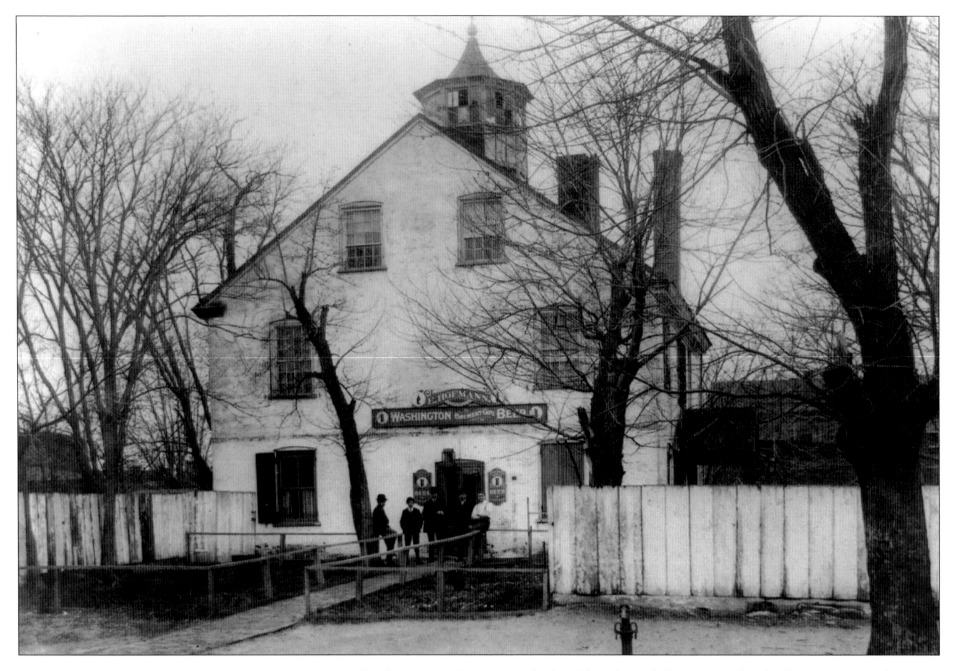

This lowly pre-1790 structure, looking like a lost lighthouse crossed with a barn, was a popular watering hole and political meeting place during the government's infancy. John Adams stopped here at least twice while overseeing the transfer of the government from Philadelphia to Washington in 1800, and it hosted the first formal ball of the city in December 1796. It was named for William Tunnicliff, its manager from 1796 through 1799. Illustrative of the dramatic rebuilding of the city, it was closed by 1821 but would be the only 18th Century hotel to survive to be photographed.

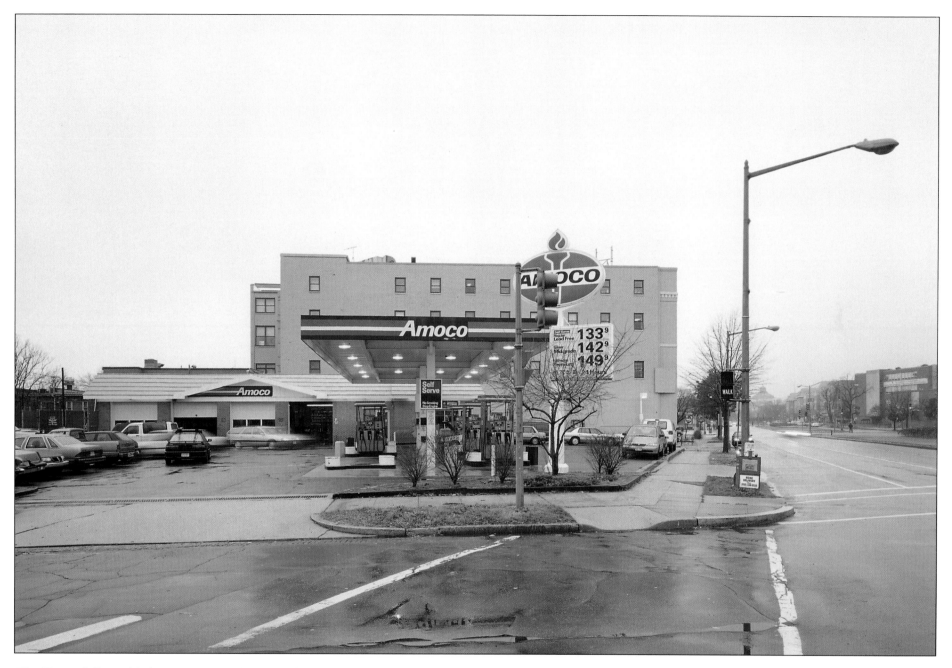

The Tunnicliff quickly became too small for a hotel, and was later used as a beer hall, a warehouse, and finally a gas station. The building was demolished in 1932, but a gas station continues to occupy the corner. A bar by the name of Tunnicliff's still operates in the neighborhood however—a very long legacy to a four-year stint as a hotel manager.

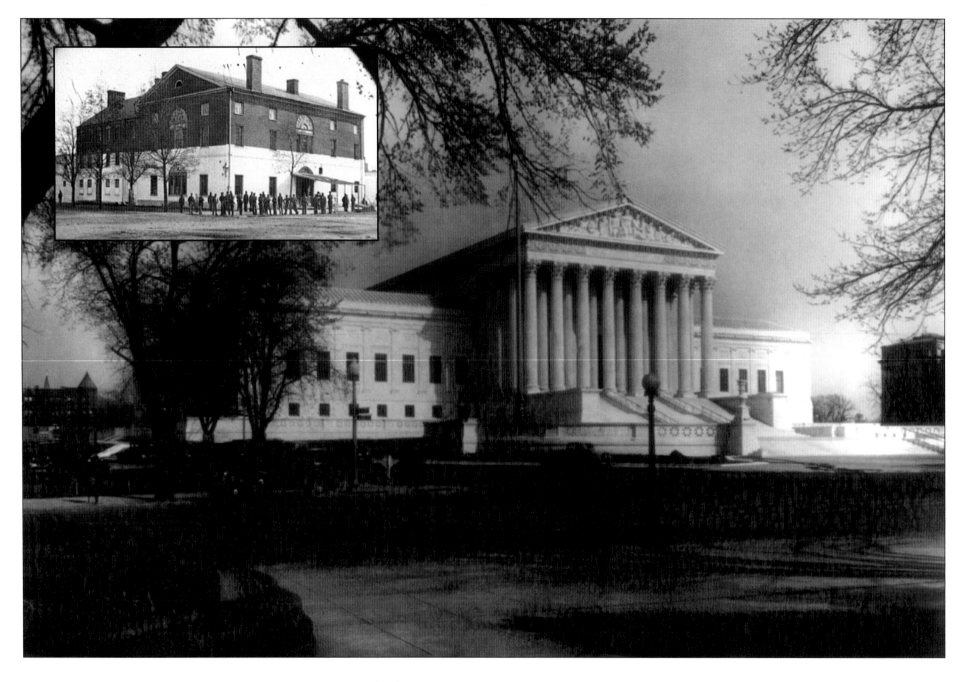

This location east of the Capitol between East Capitol Street and Maryland Avenue was the site of the "Old Brick Capitol," hastily erected to temporarily replace the burned Capitol in 1814 and used as such until 1819. The building later served as a boarding house and school until the government turned it into a Civil War prison, as shown in the inset above. It was demolished in 1867 and replaced with a row of brick houses, which were soon demolished to make way for the Supreme Court Building. The 1935 view shows the building, designed by Cass Gilbert, at its completion.

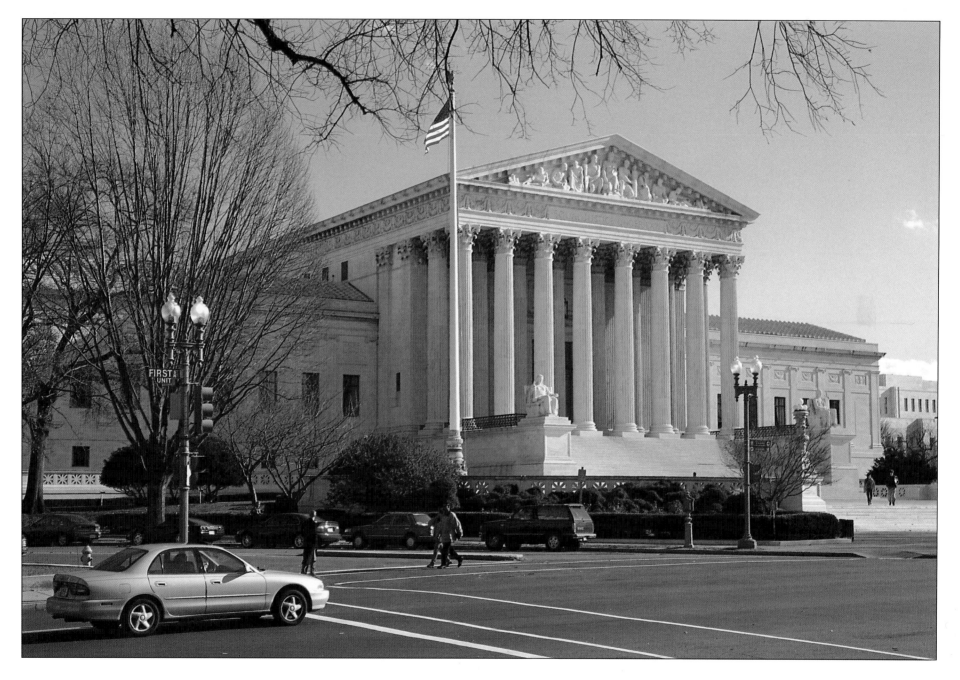

The Supreme Court, long without its own home, finally acquired one when in 1928 Congress passed the Public Buildings Act, which among other things provided for the construction of the Supreme Court Building. Today the building is the symbol of the federal government's judiciary branch, being featured regularly in newscasts and photos, and is also the scene of frequent demonstrations for or against Supreme Court decisions large and small.

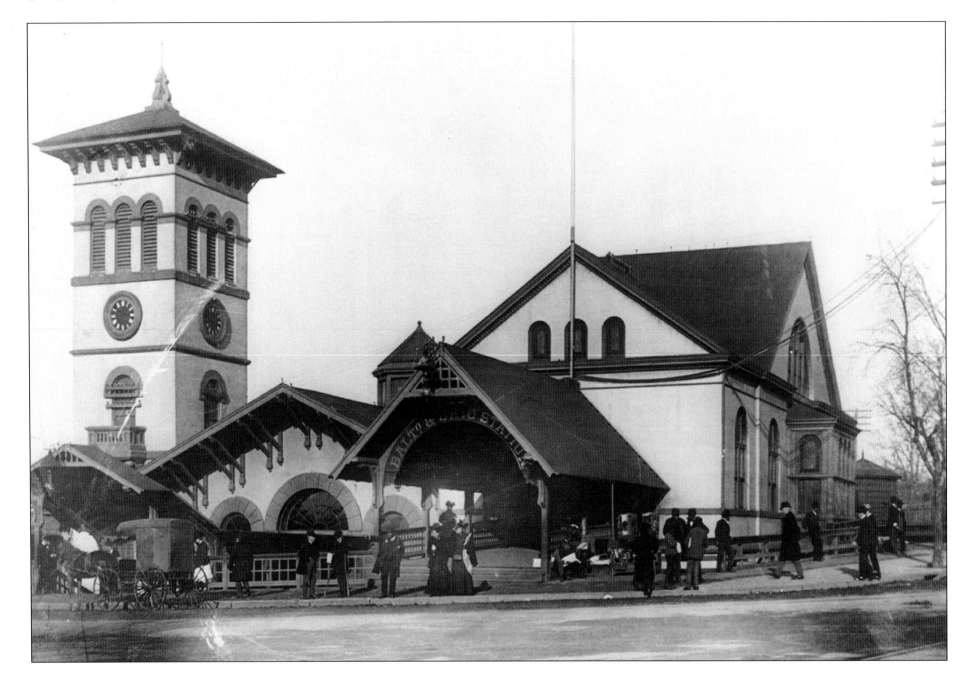

The Baltimore & Ohio Railroad was the first intercity railroad in the United States, and its first terminal in the nation's capital was built a block south of this site just blocks from Capitol Hill in 1835. This Italianate-design station, with its tracks primarily below street level, was built at C Street and New Jersey Avenue in 1850–51. The photograph above was taken around 1880. Connections to the South were originally provided with tracks down First Street and Maryland Avenue to the Long Bridge across the Potomac.

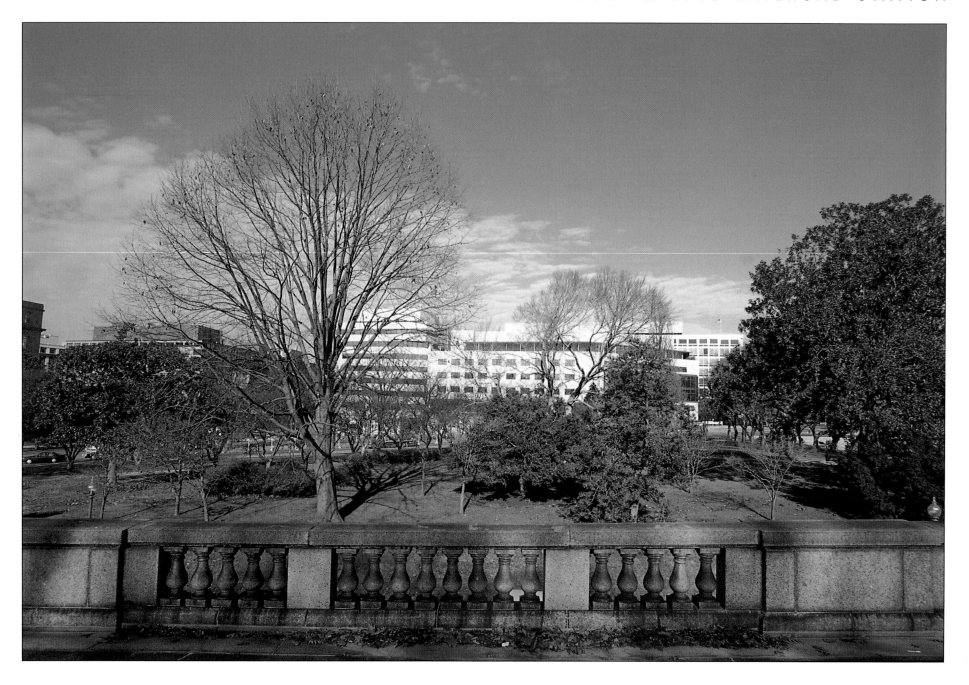

Originally seeing a modest three or four trains a day, the depot swiftly became outmoded in the later part of the century, and was demolished in 1907 when it was replaced by the newly built Union Station to the north. The area between Union Station and the Capitol became part of Union Station Plaza, under the Public Buildings Act of 1928, and the area is now open green space.

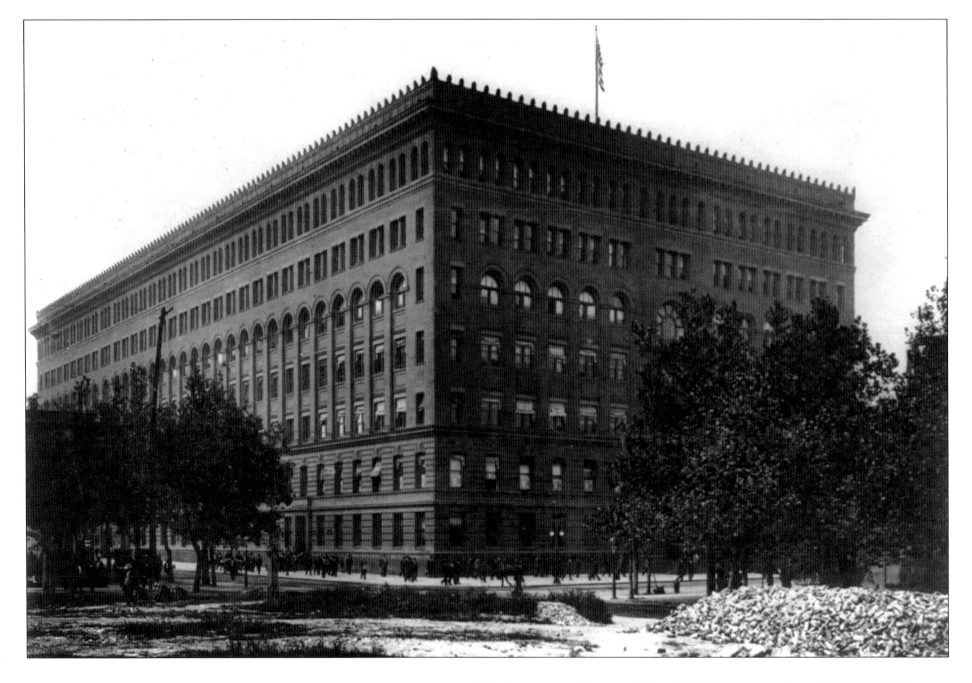

The Government Printing Office (G.P.O.) was created in 1852 to satisfy the printing needs of Congress. Authorized by Congress in 1860, it serves today as the printing arm of the U.S. government, performing nearly all printing and binding for the entire federal community. It is still regarded as the largest printing plant in the world. This photograph was taken in 1908.

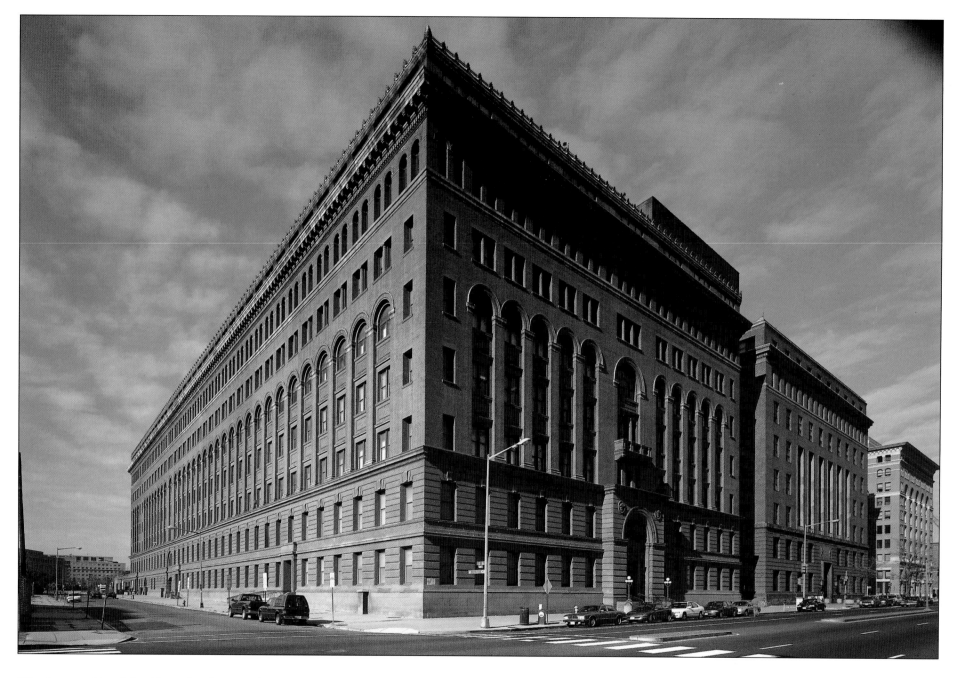

The large red brick building that houses the G.P.O. was erected in 1903 on
G and Capitol streets, and is unusual in being one of the few large, red brick
government structures in a city that now seems to be mostly marble and granite.
(The Smithsonian Castle and the Pension Building, now the National Building
Museum, are other exceptions.) An additional structure was attached to its
north in later years.

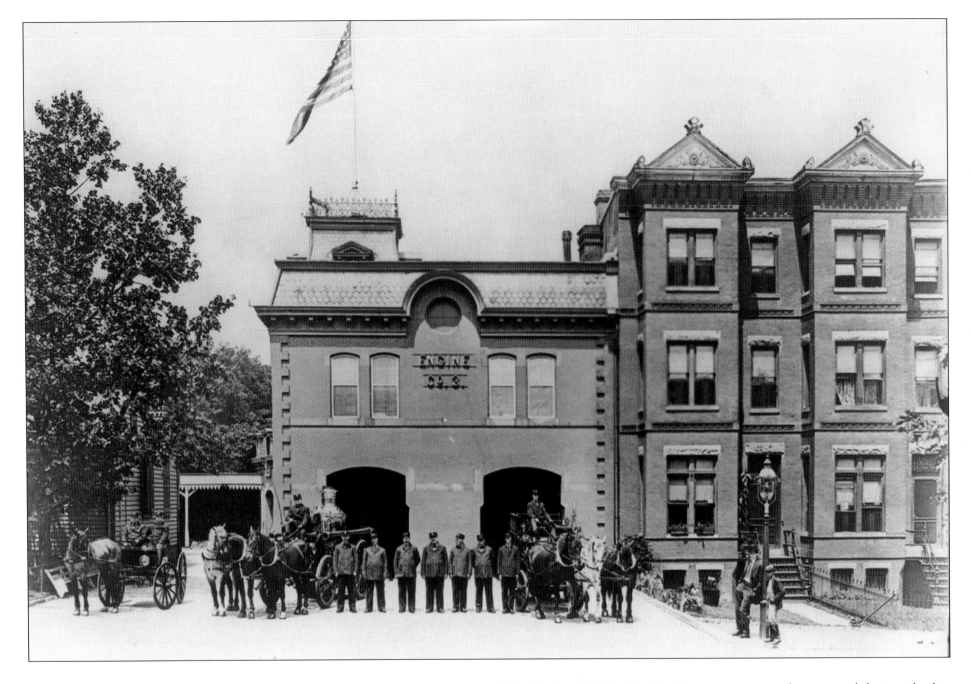

The District of Columbia Fire Department, started as a consolidation of volunteer fire departments in 1864, became fully professional under the D.C.F.D. banner in 1871. The last horse-drawn apparatus was retired in 1925. Engine 3 occupied this firehouse at C Street and Delaware Avenue, NE, between the Capitol and what became Union Station, in May 1875.

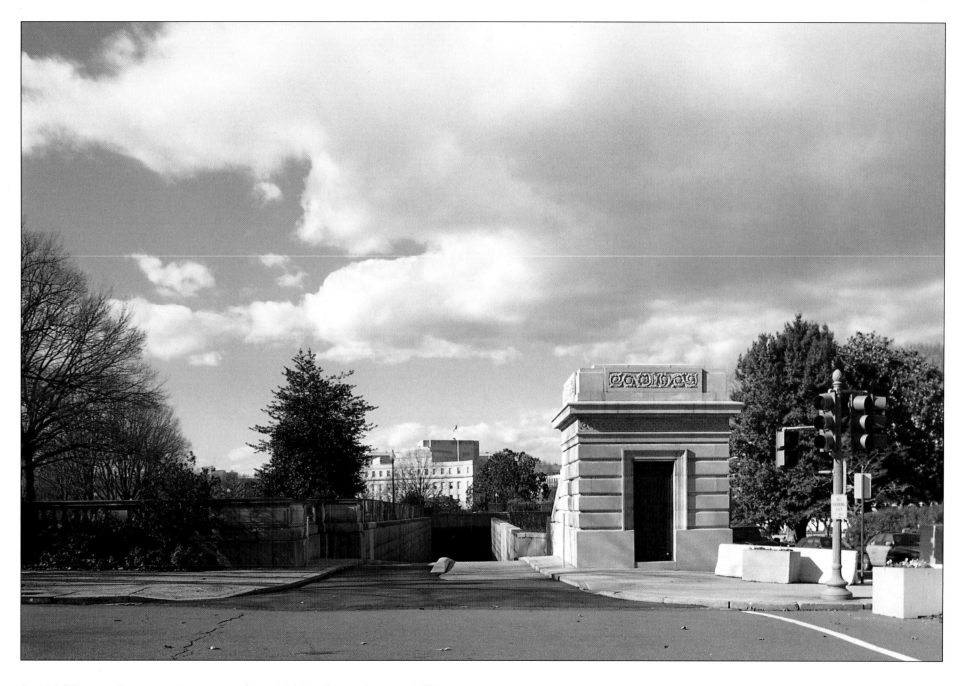

In 1916 Engine Company 3 was moved to 439 New Jersey Avenue, NW, just around the corner; that firehouse was closed in 1993. The 1928 Public Buildings Act that eliminated most structures between Union Station and the Capitol also eliminated this firehouse, and today the location looks at an entrance to the underground parking garage of the Russell Senate Office Building.

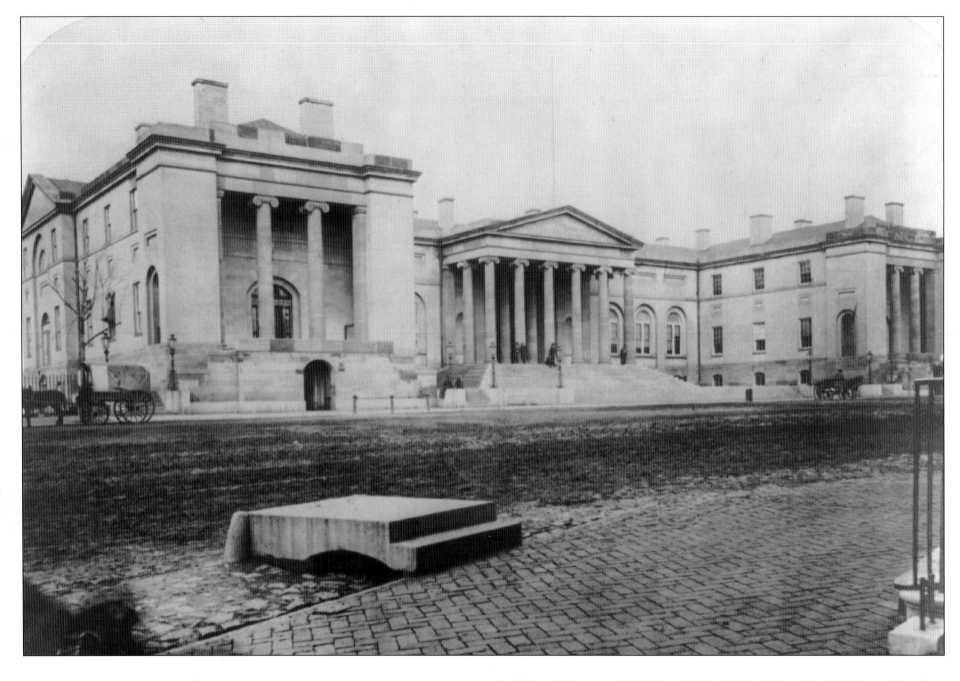

At 4th and D streets, NW, the old City Hall, designed by British architect George Hadfield, was begun in 1820 but was completed in 1853 without the planned central dome. A lottery plan failed to raise enough capital to finish the structure and the federal government allocated funds for its completion, with the condition that it be permitted to occupy one wing when it was finished, which it used for circuit and criminal courts.

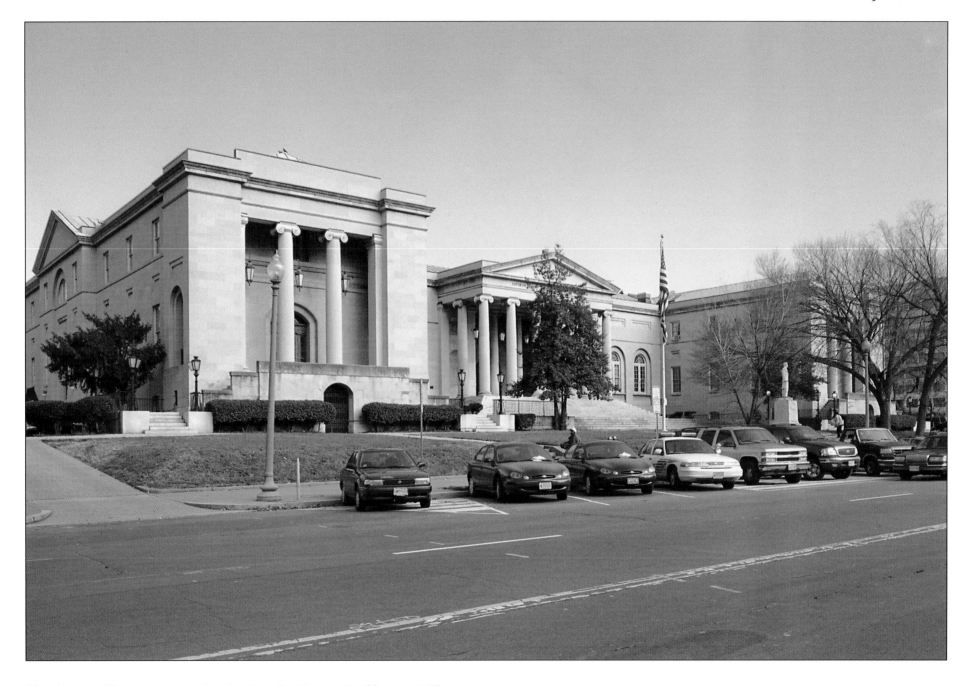

The district offices were moved in 1908 to the District Building, at 14th Street and Pennsylvania Avenue, NW, and the old City Hall stands today in the heart of Judiciary Square, still used by the government of the District of Columbia and the U.S. Circuit Court.

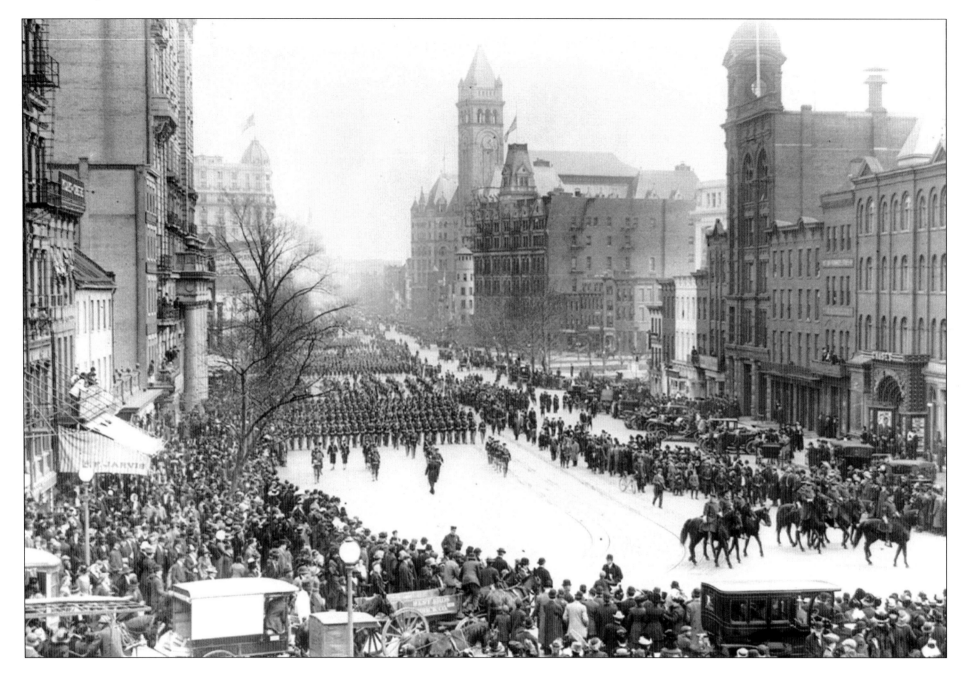

The avenue between the White House and Capitol has hosted parades triumphant and somber over the years. (The latter is shown with the funeral of victims of the U.S.S. *Maine* explosion of 1896 on page 134.) The massive edifice in the center of both of these photographs is the Main Post Office, now the third tallest building in Washington (including the Washington Monument) at 315 feet. Rising to the right is the clock tower of the Southern Railway Building, which was completed in 1903 but destroyed by fire in 1916, four years after this photograph was taken.

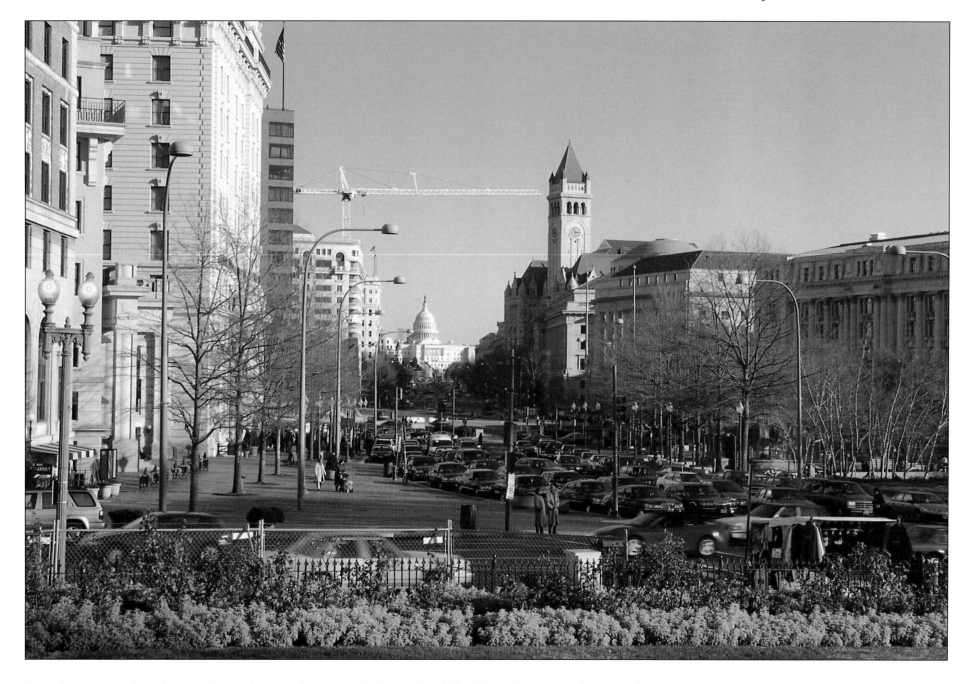

The classic view of Washington's grand avenue between the Capitol and the White House is still obtained from the steps of the Treasury Building at 15th Street. The modern view shows the Willard Hotel on the left, with Freedom Plaza (renamed in 1988 from Western Plaza) disrupting the grand avenue view in the foreground and Federal Triangle lining almost the whole of the right side of Pennsylvania Avenue.

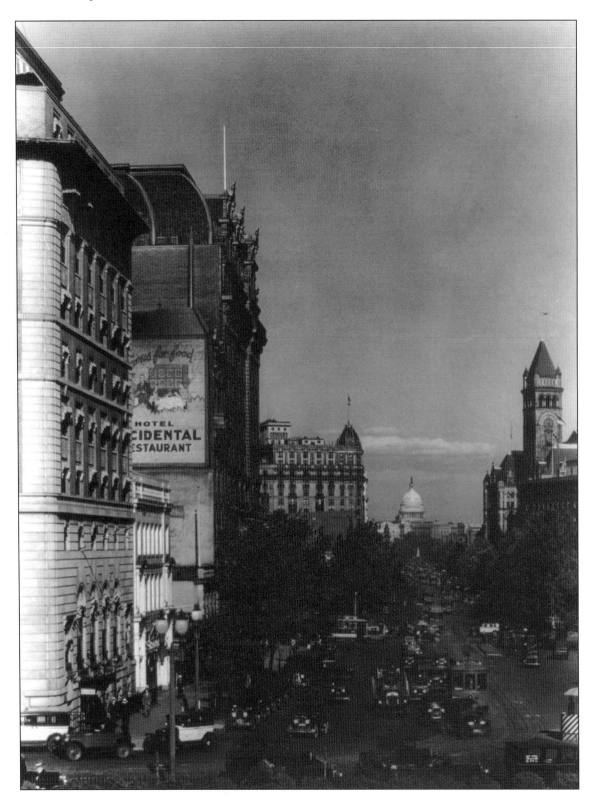

Dating to about 1930, this later view down Pennsylvania Avenue just predates the pending Federal Triangle project, and shows the refurbished Willard Hotel at right center. The Occidental Restaurant, advertised on the billboard, was a noted feature of the Willard since 1906, and sported hundreds of autographed celebrity and politician photographs on its walls; it survives today as the Occidental Grill.

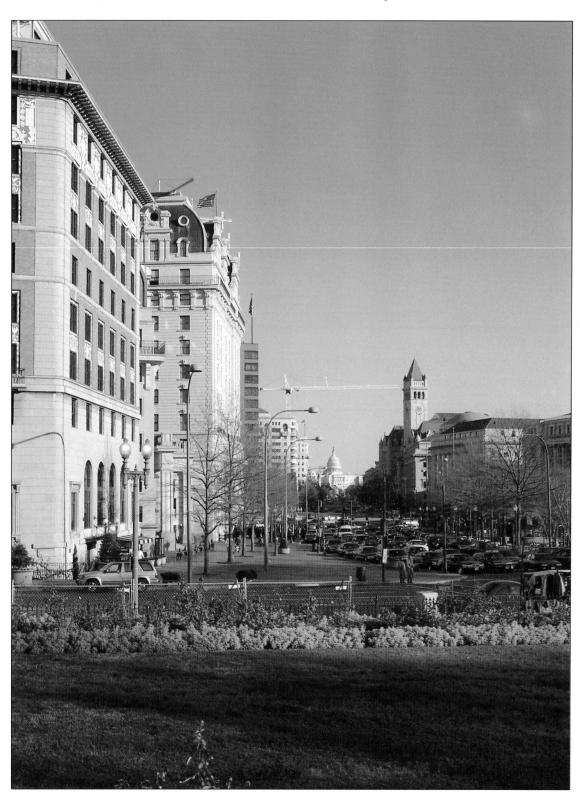

By the 1960s, Pennsylvania Avenue had become an embarrassing mess of tourist and pawn shops and dilapidated buildings blending with the majestic federal buildings. Planned redevelopment occurred over the years to restore much of the grandeur of the avenue in the present scene.

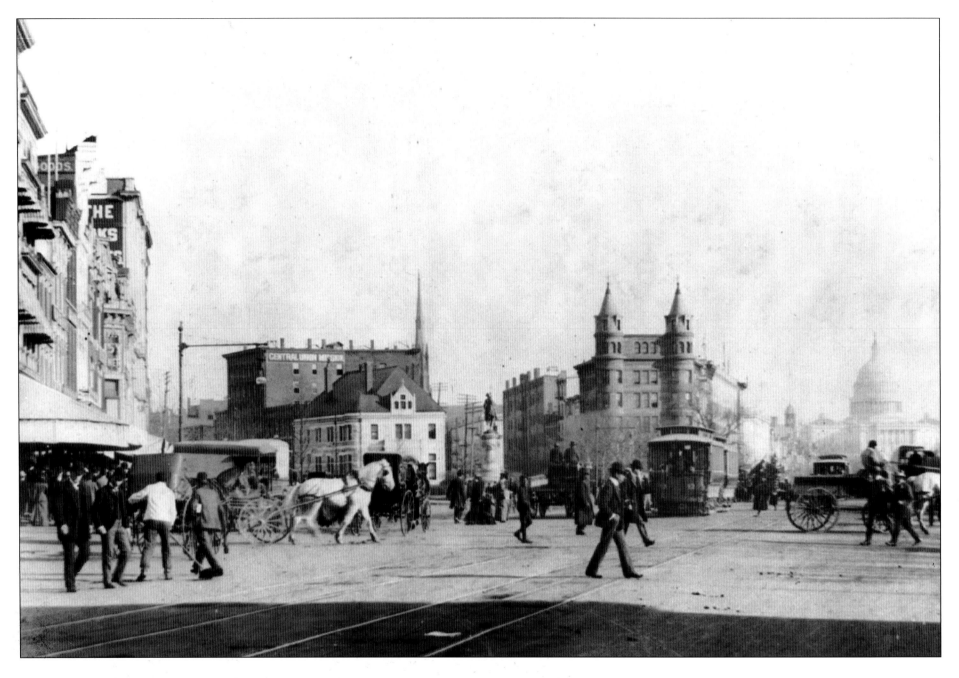

This overall view of Pennsylvania Avenue depicts pedestrian traffic that would be almost unthinkable today. Note the white-coated street-sweeper to the left. The twin-towered building to the right of center was known as the Central National Bank building and was erected in 1888. Another bank was erected in the building to its left in 1889; just down Pennsylvania Avenue from it sits the studio building of early photographer Matthew Brady, now legendary for his Civil War photography.

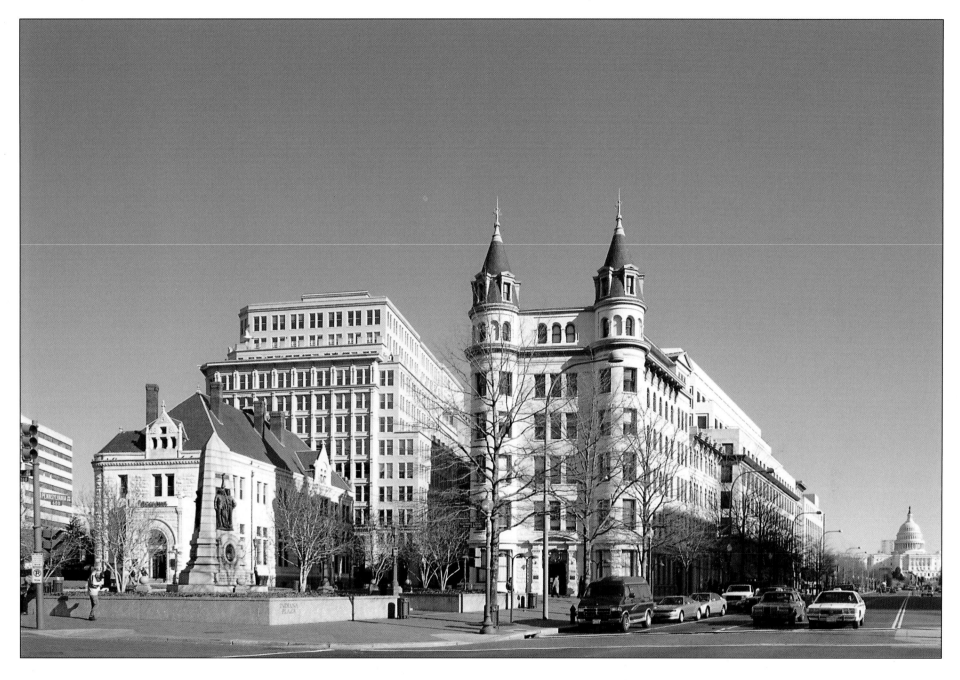

To the left in the modern photograph is the granite and bronze monument to the Grand Army of the Republic's founder Benjamin F. Stephenson, M.D., erected in 1909 by the G.A.R., which sits on what is now Indiana Plaza. The twin-towered building is now used by the National Council of Negro Women; the other bank building is still used by the Riggs National Bank.

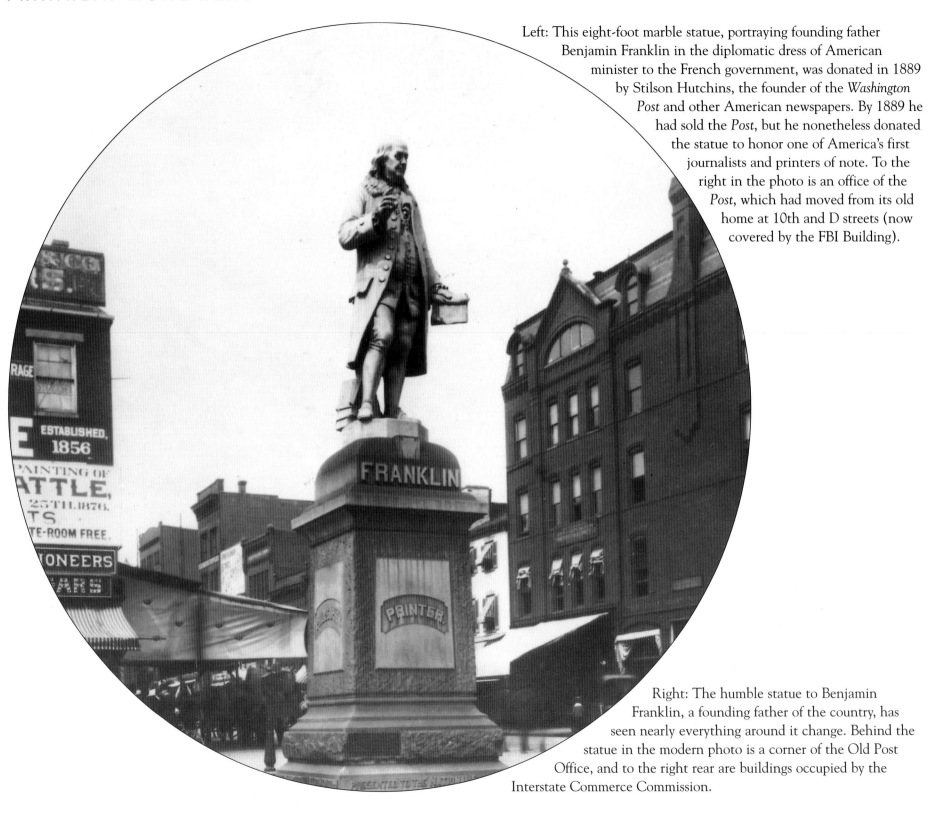

Left: This eight-foot marble statue, portraying founding father Benjamin Franklin in the diplomatic dress of American minister to the French government, was donated in 1889 by Stilson Hutchins, the founder of the *Washington Post* and other American newspapers. By 1889 he had sold the *Post*, but he nonetheless donated the statue to honor one of America's first journalists and printers of note. To the right in the photo is an office of the *Post*, which had moved from its old home at 10th and D streets (now covered by the FBI Building).

Right: The humble statue to Benjamin Franklin, a founding father of the country, has seen nearly everything around it change. Behind the statue in the modern photo is a corner of the Old Post Office, and to the right rear are buildings occupied by the Interstate Commerce Commission.

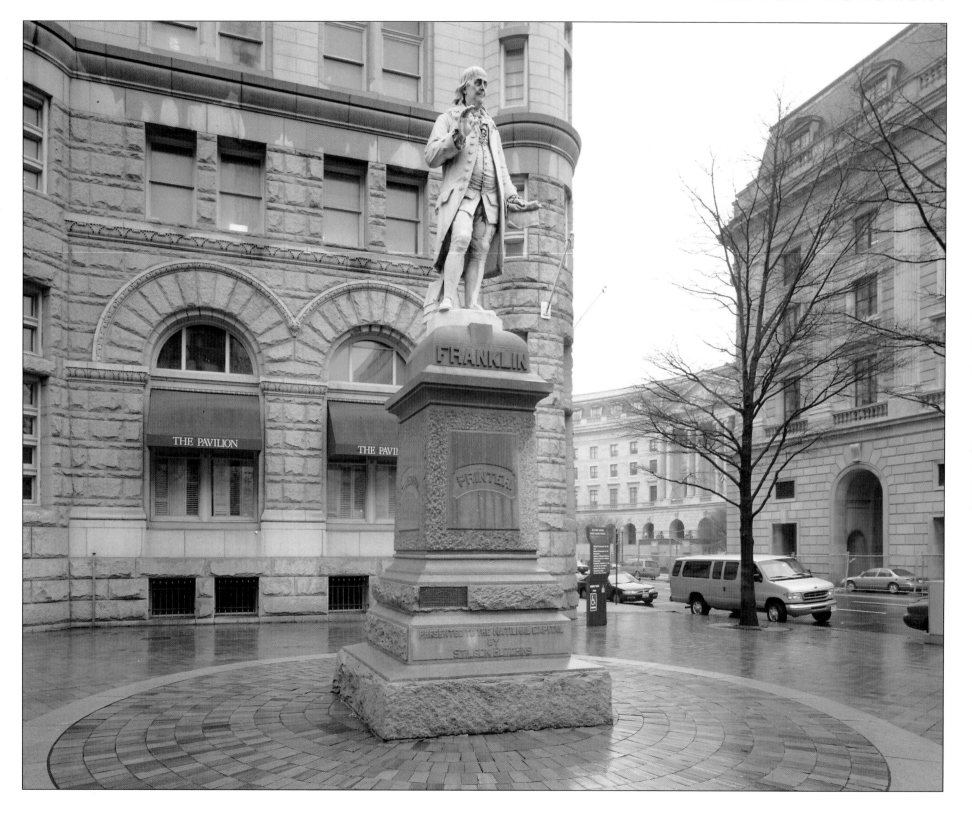

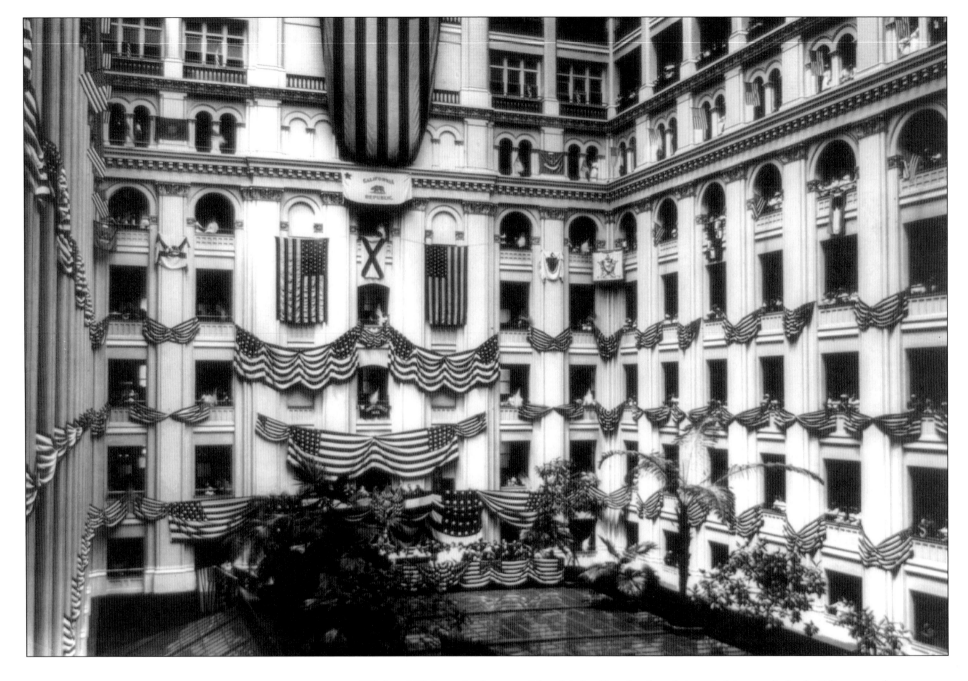

With a 315-foot clock tower (the third-tallest landmark in Washington) the building now known as the Old Post Office was built in 1899 to serve as both the main city post office (1898–1914, replaced by a new Post Office across the street from Union Station) and offices of the U.S. Post Office Department (1899–1934). Noted for its elaborate Flag Day pageantry and displays, it was the first Federal building along Pennsylvania Avenue between the White House and Capitol, and the first in what would eventually become Federal Triangle. This photo shows a Flag Day display circa 1910.

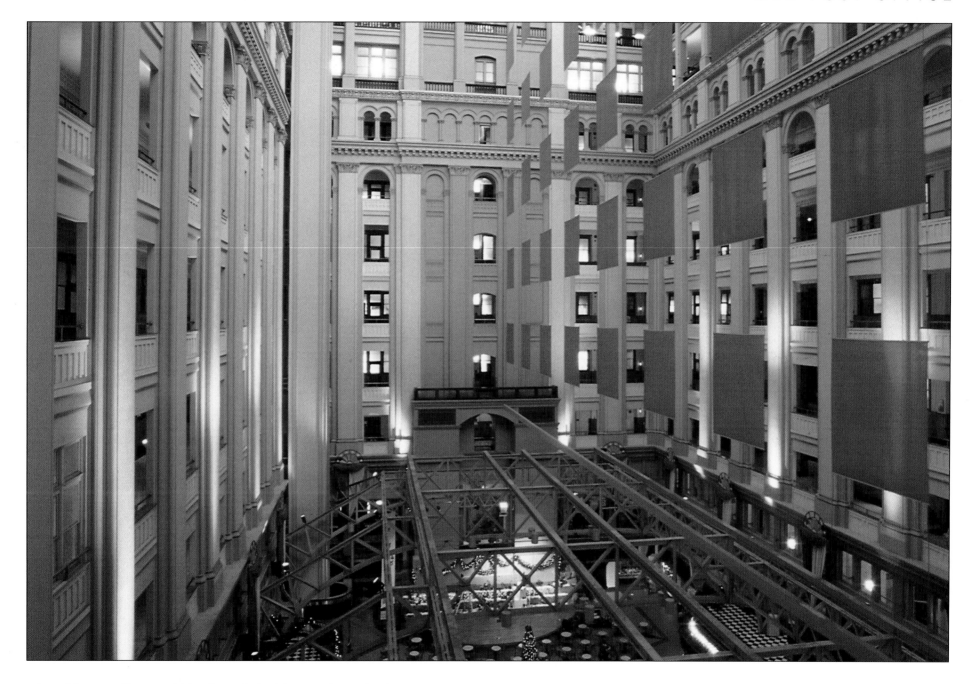

The Old Post Office would be the only building in the Federal Triangle to survive the reconstruction of neoclassical Federal buildings throughout the area. After numerous occupants and threats to demolish the structure, preservationists were successful in saving the building and it was renovated in 1978–83 for combined commercial and office use. It now houses the National Endowment for the Humanities and a shopping court.

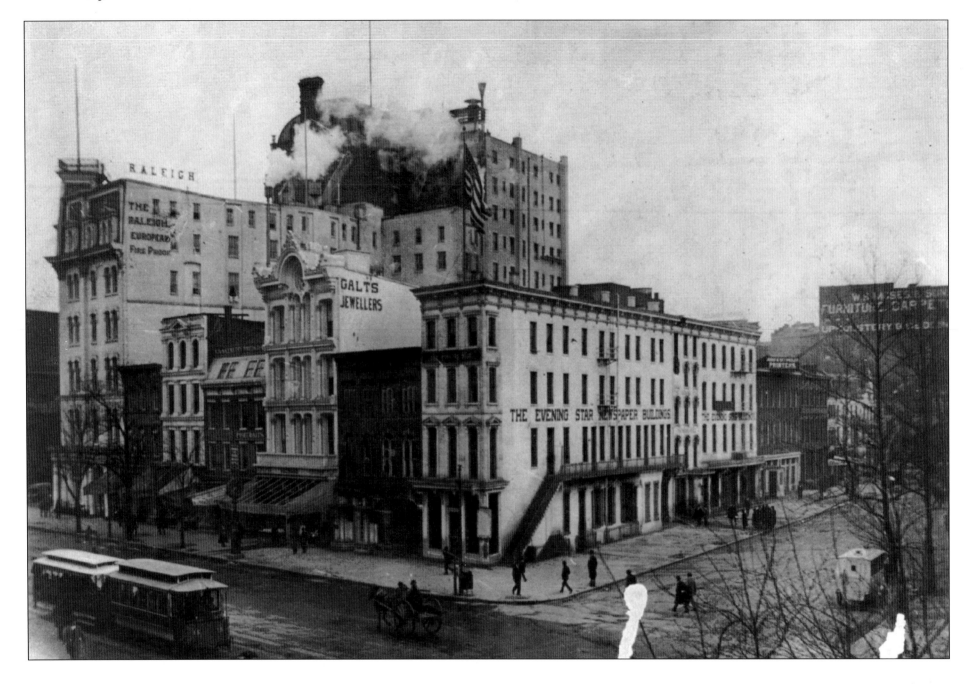

This view from about 1890 shows the haphazard architecture typical of the post-Civil War Pennsylvania Avenue on a section that housed a great many newspaper offices. Prominent on the near corner is the office of the Washington *Evening Star*, which was founded in 1852 and occupied a building on the southwest corner of this intersection from 1854 to 1881. It then moved around this side of Pennsylvania Avenue in various buildings until 1898, when it constructed the building that now stands on this corner.

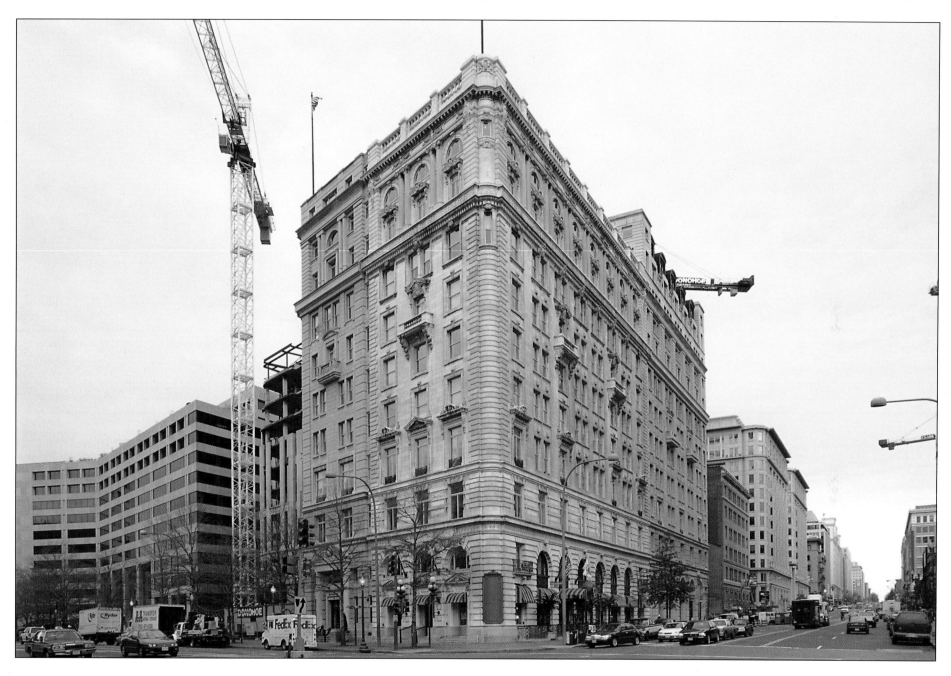

The *Evening Star* itself outlived a hundred other newspapers in the city, but finally folded in 1981, a victim of declining evening newspaper circulation nationwide. The building continues to be known as the Evening Star Building, even though it now houses offices and has added its next-door neighbor. On the 11th Street side can be seen the entrance to a Planet Hollywood restaurant; construction is ongoing on a new office complex, to be known as 1111 Pennsylvania Avenue, at the other corner to the left.

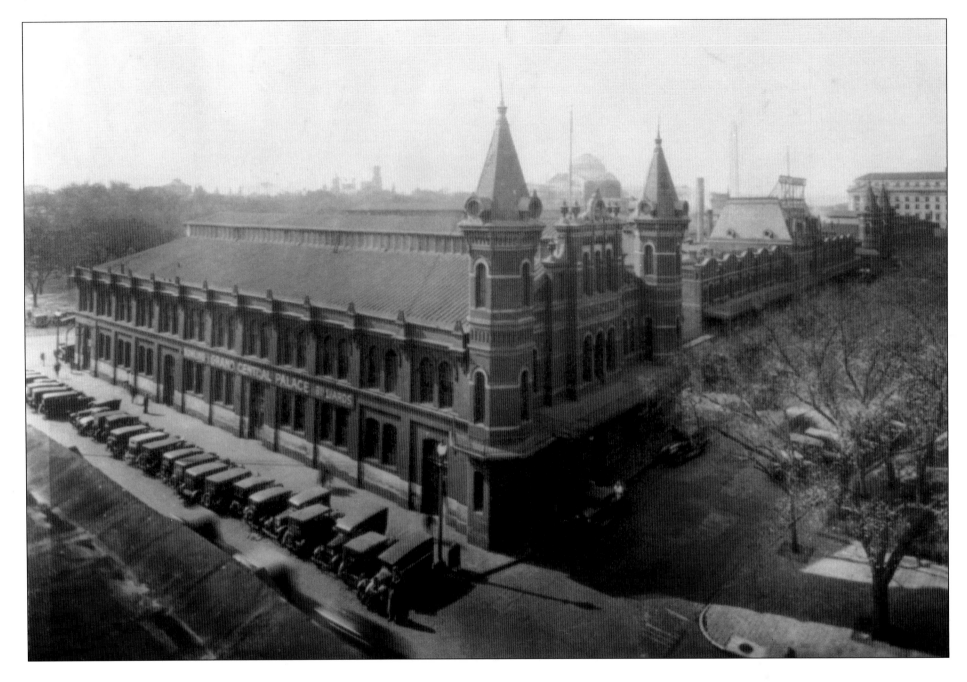

Central Market was the largest of five major markets in the city (of which only Eastern Market, at 7th Street and South Carolina Avenue, SE, survives at this time) and among the largest market houses in the nation, offering space for up to 300 vendors and their wagons. Designed by Adolph Cluss and built in 1871–73 on the site of the city's primary market site since its beginnings, it was conveniently located on the Washington Canal (now Constitution Avenue), permitting daily delivery of fresh produce.

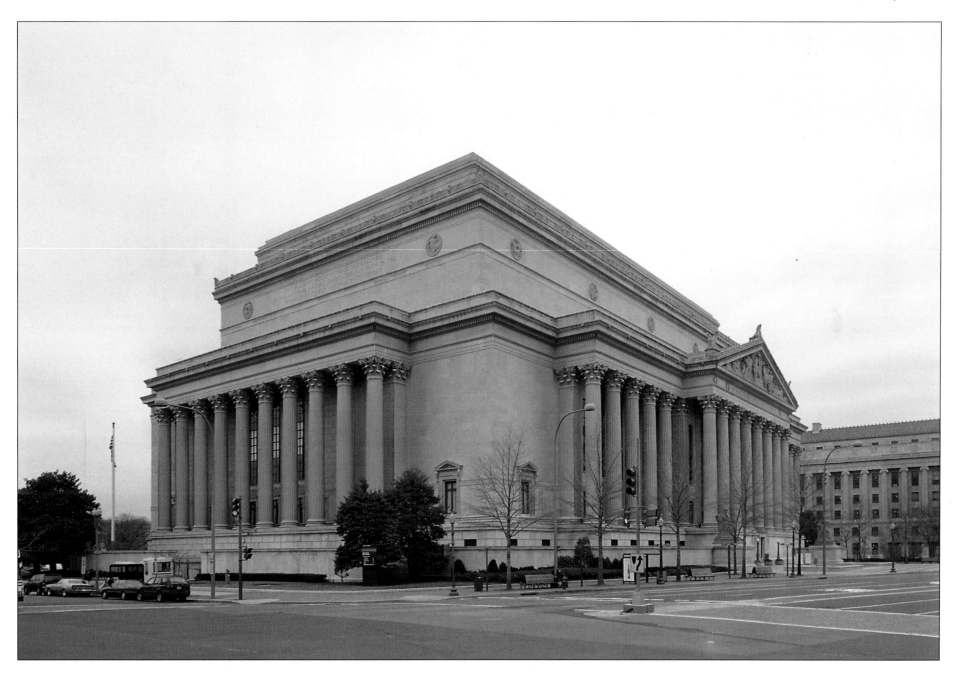

The Central Market had largely been replaced by corner stores, and later supermarkets, when it was demolished in 1931 as part of the Federal Triangle redevelopment project. The National Archives was built on the site in 1931–34 and houses the original Declaration of Indepenence, the U.S. Constitution, and the Bill of Rights.

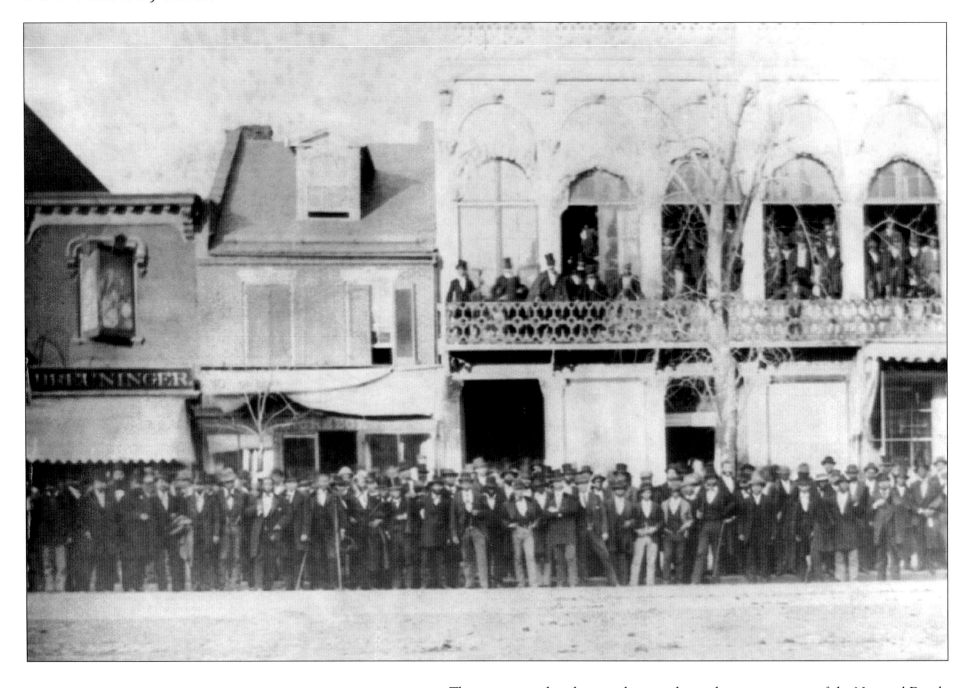

The caption on this photograph states that it depicts a meeting of the National Equal Rights Convention, at the Metzerott Hotel at 925 Pennsylvania Avenue in Washington, D.C., on December 9, 1873. Regrettably, no information could be found on this meeting; it would take until 1910 for the National Association for the Advancement of Colored People, now the largest and most significant civil-rights group in America, to be founded.

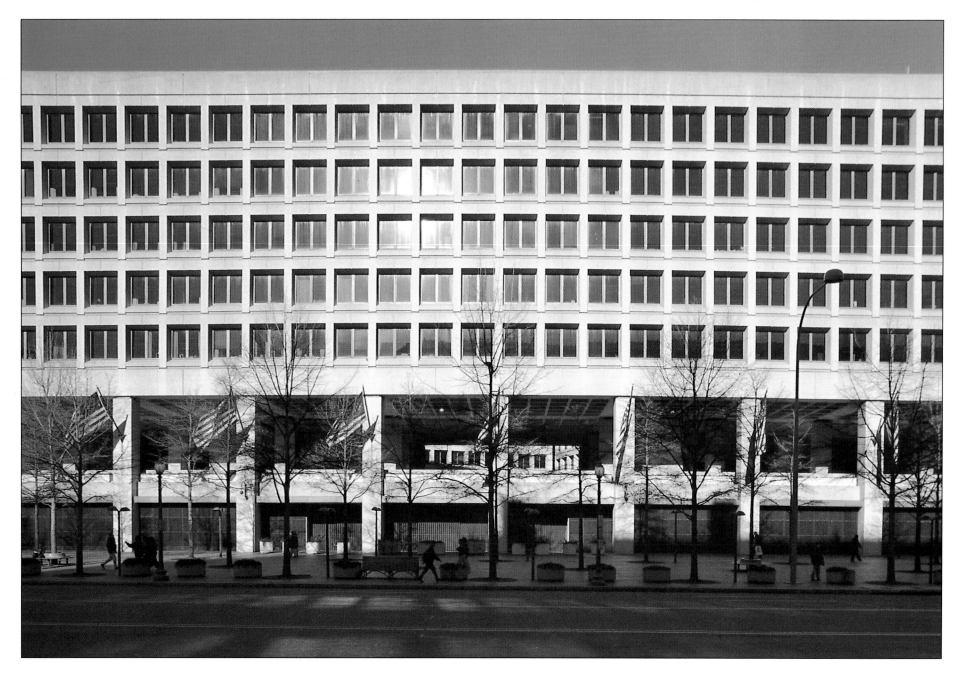

At the location today is the much-maligned J. Edgar Hoover Building of the Federal Bureau of Investigation, opened in 1974, with a design (frequently referred to sarcastically as "neo-Brutalism") that is totally inconsistent with the Federal Triangle district across the street. The building's erection at the site may be regarded as considerably ironic, given Hoover's record (or lack thereof) on civil rights during the 1960s.

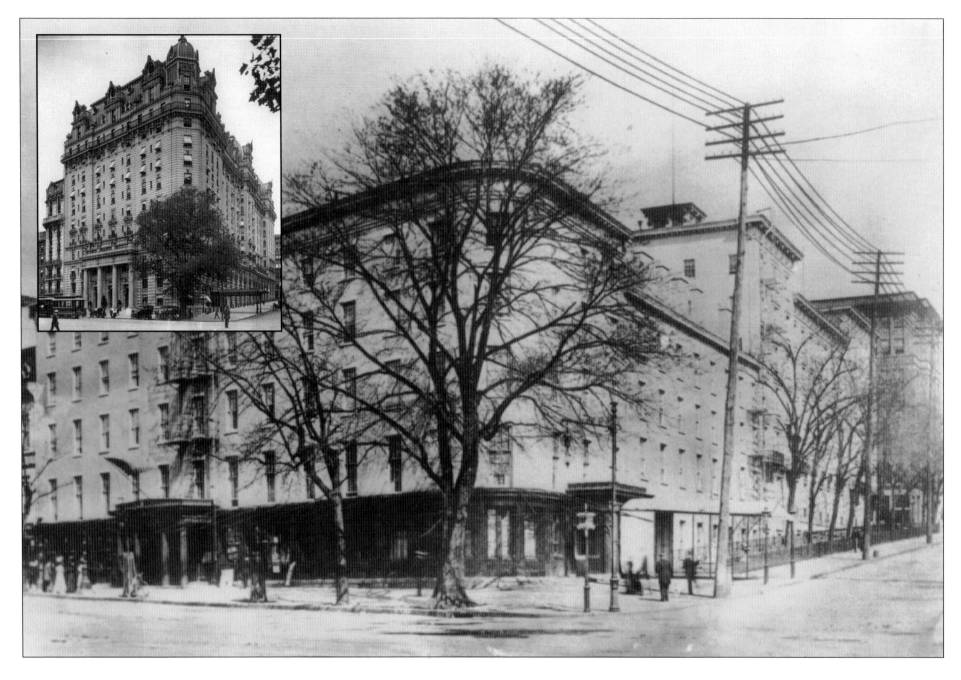

Originally founded as the City Hotel, at 14th Street and Pennsylvania Avenue, NW, in 1816 by Benjamin Ogle Tayloe, the Willard would be named after Henry Willard, who took over the hotel in the 1850s. Due to its central location and proximity to the White House, it became a center of political and social activity for decades. Among the famous short-term occupants were Charles Dickens (in 1842) and presidents Taylor, Fillmore, Buchanan, and Lincoln. In 1861, Julia Ward Howe wrote "The Battle Hymn of the Republic" while staying at the hotel. The term "lobbyists" was supposedly coined by President Grant to refer to power brokers that continually courted him in the Willard's lobby. The old building in the front of the photograph was expanded with newly built sections uphill and to the right in 1858.

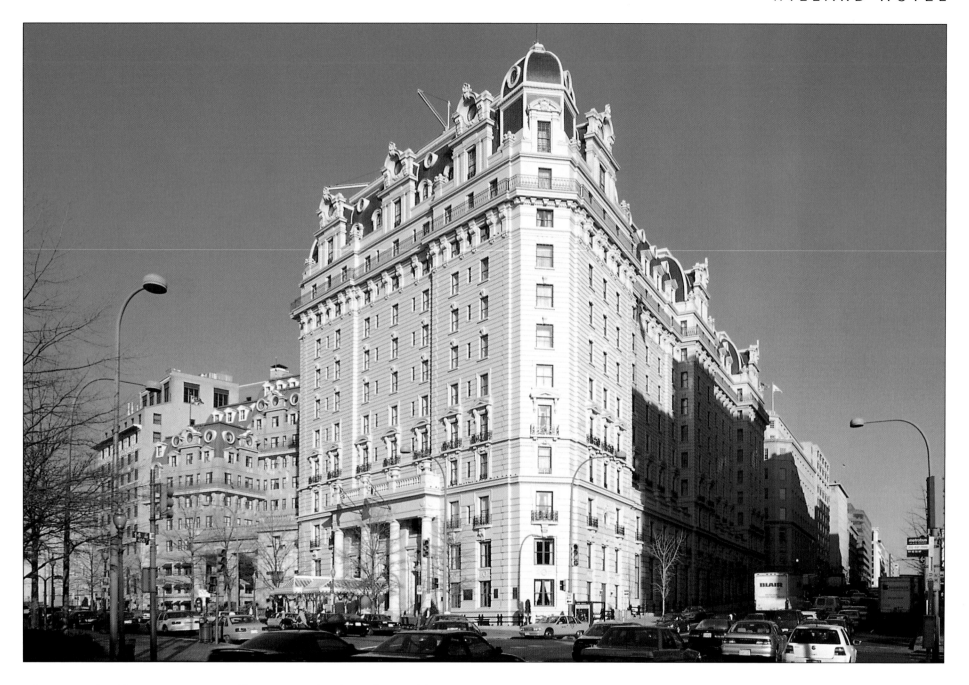

The current building was constructed here in 1901 and was designed by Henry Hardenbergh, who also designed New York's Plaza and Waldorf-Astoria hotels. Martin Luther King, Jr., wrote his epic "I Have a Dream" speech here before delivering it at the Lincoln Memorial in August 1963. The hotel fell upon hard times after World War II, closing in 1968 and remaining empty until 1986, when it reopened after an extensive renovation; it remains an active hotel today.

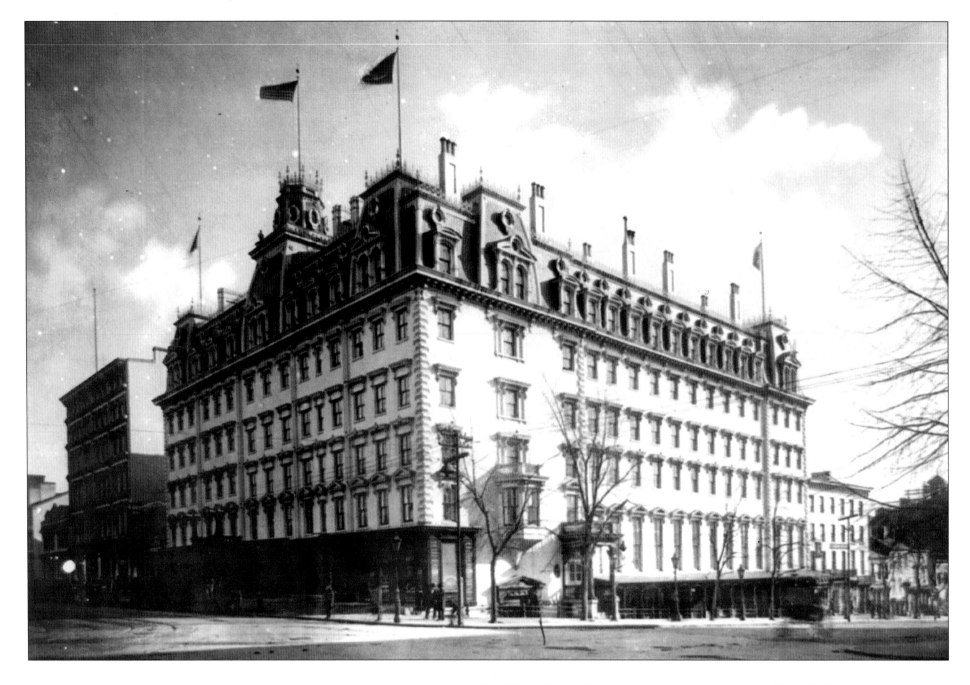

The Ebbitt House Hotel, on the southeast corner of 14th & F streets (across the street from the Willard), distinguished itself by being the first hotel in Washington to remain open all summer instead of closing when Congress adjourned. It was demolished in 1925 and the National Press Building was erected on the site in 1926. The latter fell upon hard times during the great Depression but rebounded after World War II, hosting offices, shops, and a theater.

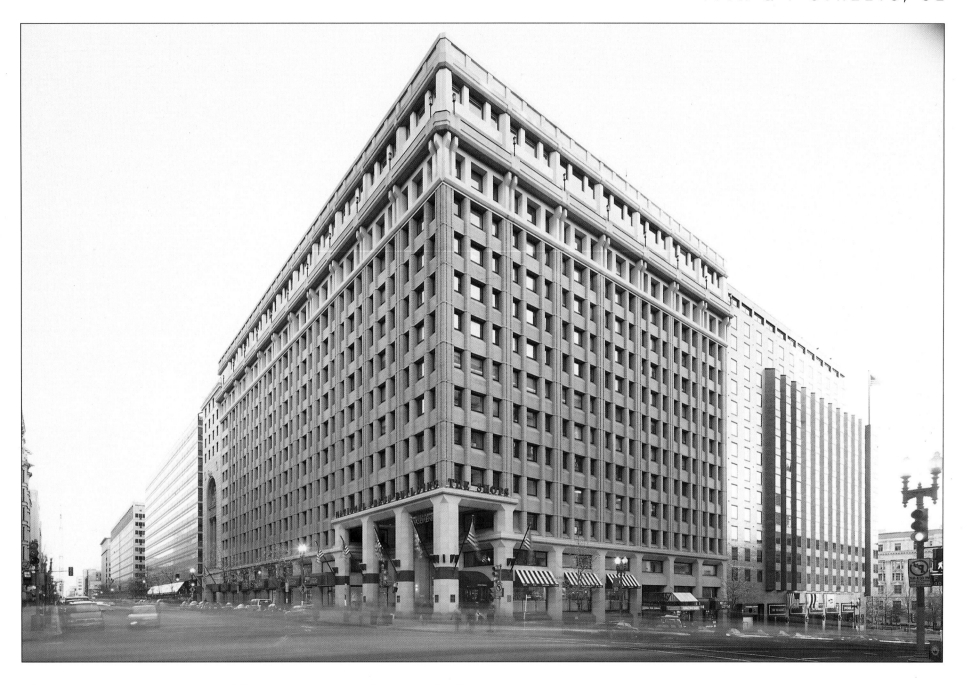

The building was later reconstructed, beginning in 1982, adding a popular shopping mall but altering the original façade. World leaders and dignitaries from Churchill to Gandhi to Lindbergh to various presidents have visited the Press Club that occupies the top floor. The building also covers the site (1336–38 F Street) of the Washington home of Aaron Burr, Jefferson's vice president, who killed Alexander Hamilton in a duel in 1804.

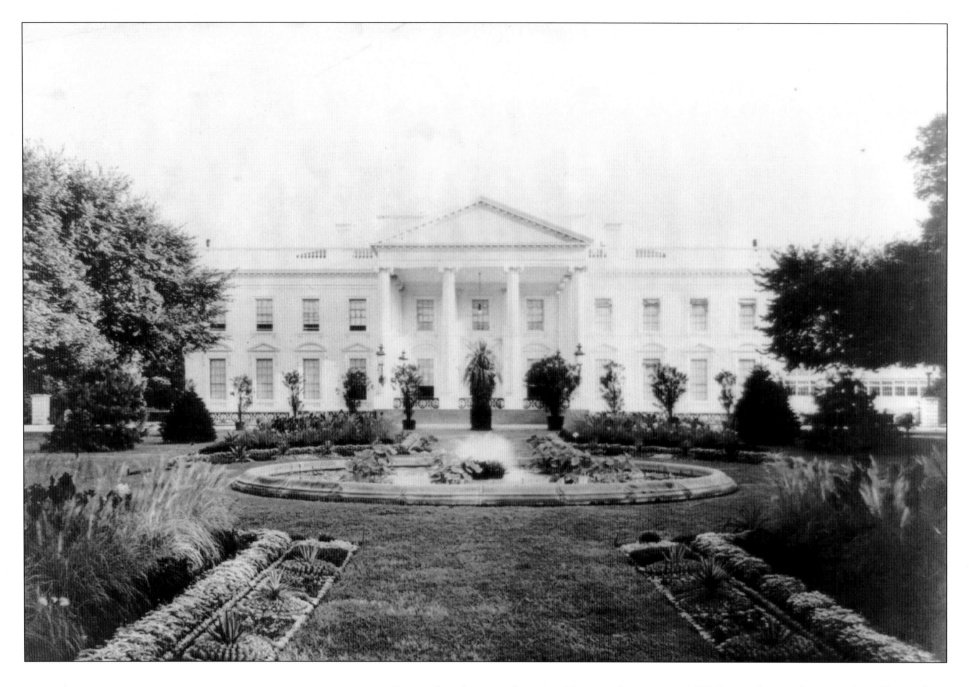

Located at the most famous address in the nation, 1600 Pennsylvania Avenue, the oldest public building in Washington at first looks little changed from its original design by James Hoban, based on country estate houses in Britain and Ireland. However, many changes have occurred. Officially called the Executive Mansion for its first century, construction began in 1793 and was complete enough for John Adams to move in at the end of his term in 1800. It was rebuilt under Hoban's supervision between 1815 and 1817 after its torching by the British in 1814.

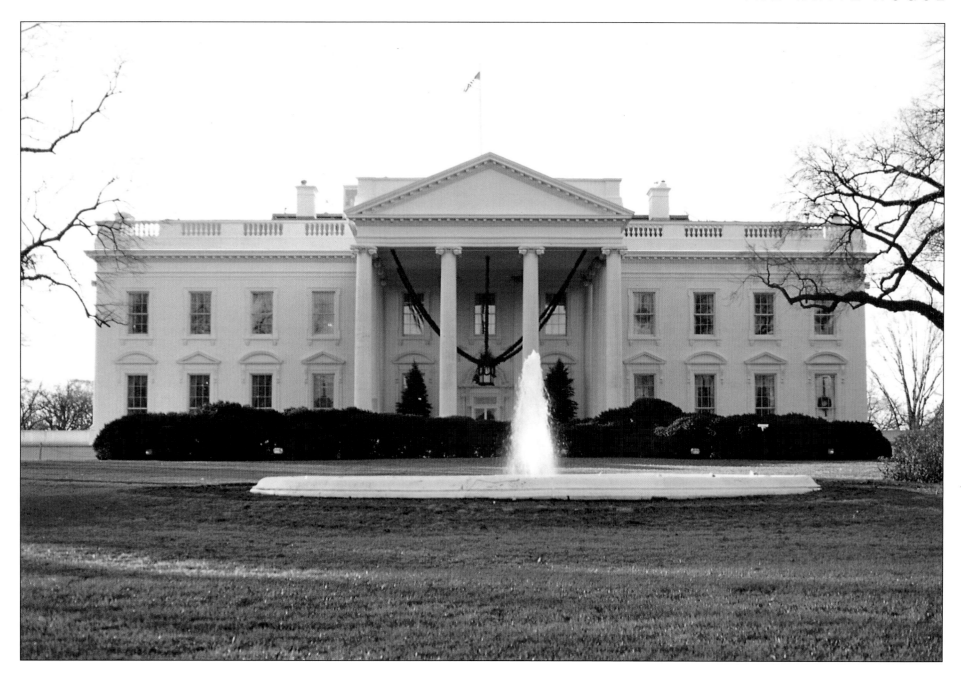

Over the years, successive occupants of the White House have made additions and refurnishings as progress allowed, including gas lighting (seen in the old view of the north portico), central heating, plumbing, and electricity. President Theodore Roosevelt officially changed the name of the residence to the White House in 1901 and undertook a major reconstruction of the interior in 1902. Also changed frequently was the landscaping surrounding the building, as seen in these two views of the North Lawn.

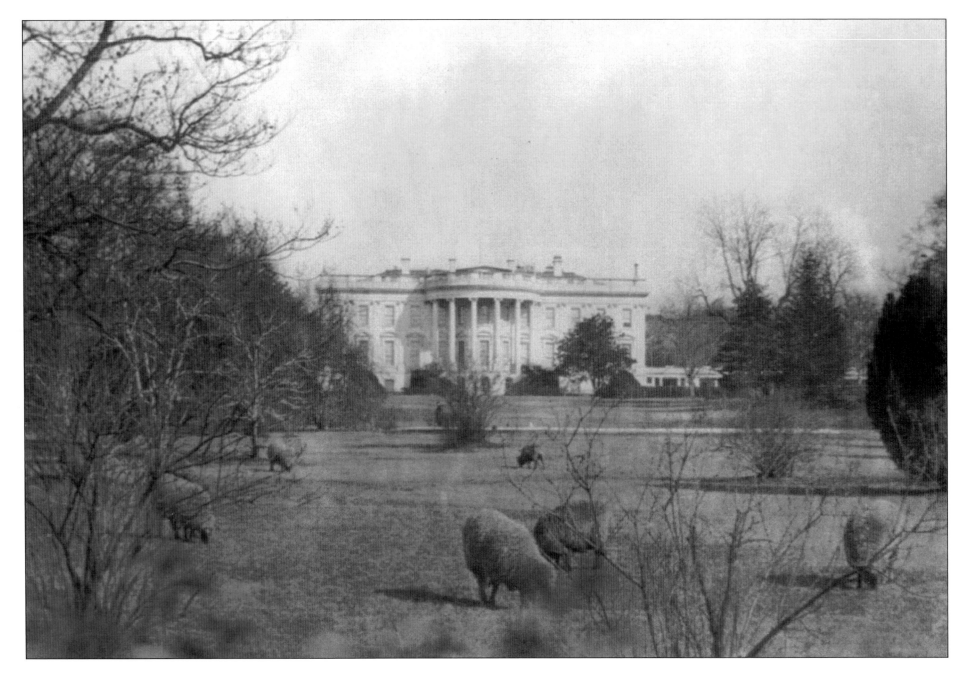

During World War I, a herd of sheep were permitted to live on the White House South Lawn, ostensibly for propaganda as much as the contribution they made to the war-thinned wool supplies. More significant modifications continued on the building over the years, including the addition of the Rose Garden in 1913, a third floor for more living space (mostly hidden behind the rooftop railings) in 1927, and an East Wing in 1942.

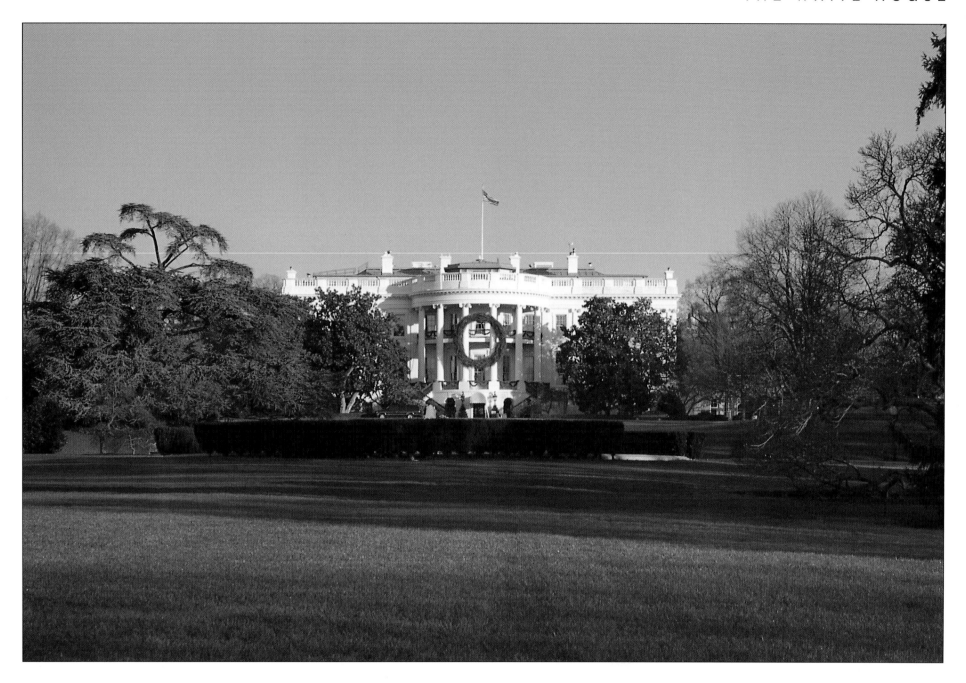

A 1948 examination under the Truman Administration revealed such severe deterioration that Truman moved across the street to Blair House while a complete interior reconstruction was undertaken, with steel and concrete replacing wood and masonry. The balcony seen on the South Portico was also added at the time. Today the White House enters its third century as the symbol of the executive branch of the United States Government, with more redecorating occurring with each successive occupant.

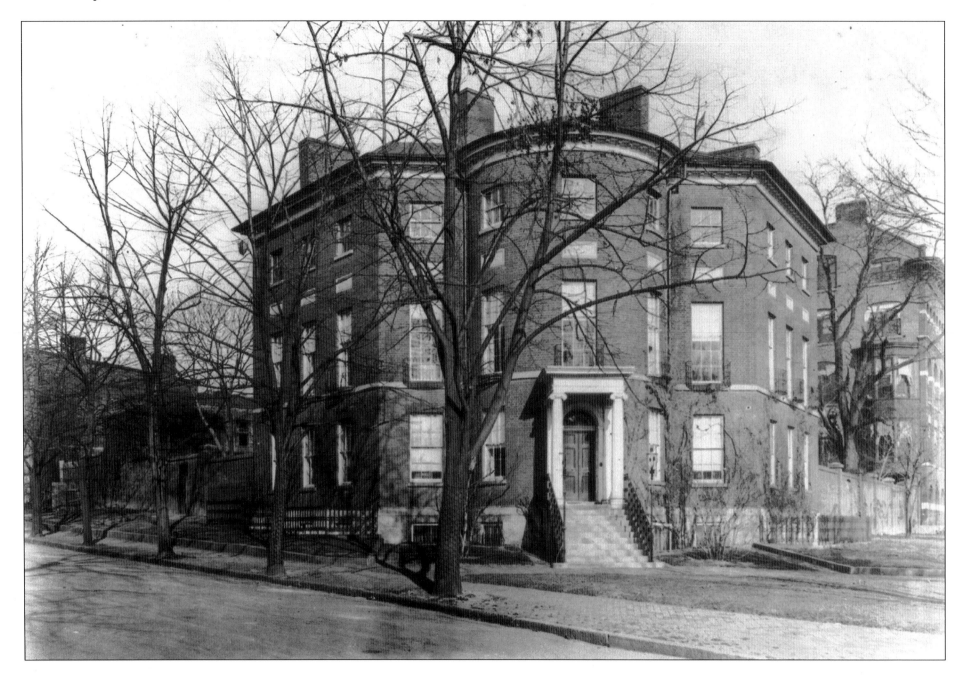

The Octagon House, also known as the Dolley Madison House, was designed by William Thornton and built by John Tayloe III in 1799 for the princely sum of $26,000—twice the estimates. The house, at 1741 New York Avenue, NW, became the temporary residence of James and Dolley Madison after the burning of the White House by the British in August 1814. The Treaty of Ghent, which ended the war with Britain and formed the basis of British-American relations for the next 180 years, was signed in the main parlor room above the entrance on February 17, 1815. This photograph dates from 1913.

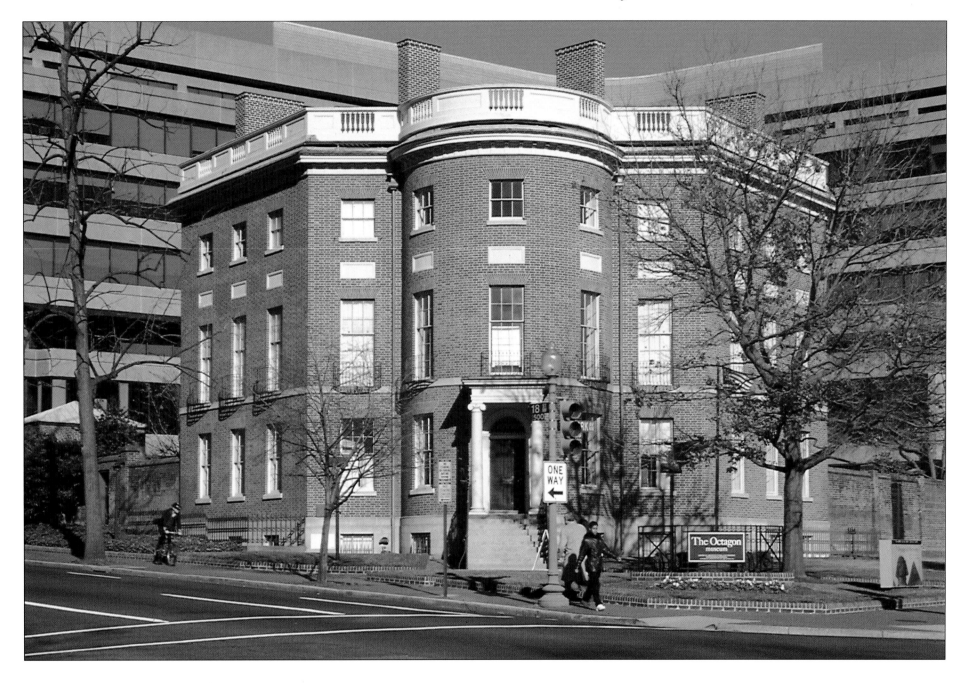

The Octagon House became the home of the American Institute of Architects in 1899. In 1965, the A.I.A. sold the Octagon to its nonprofit arm, now known as The American Architectural Foundation, which operates a museum in the building. The building to the rear, opened in 1973, now holds the expanded offices of the A.I.A.

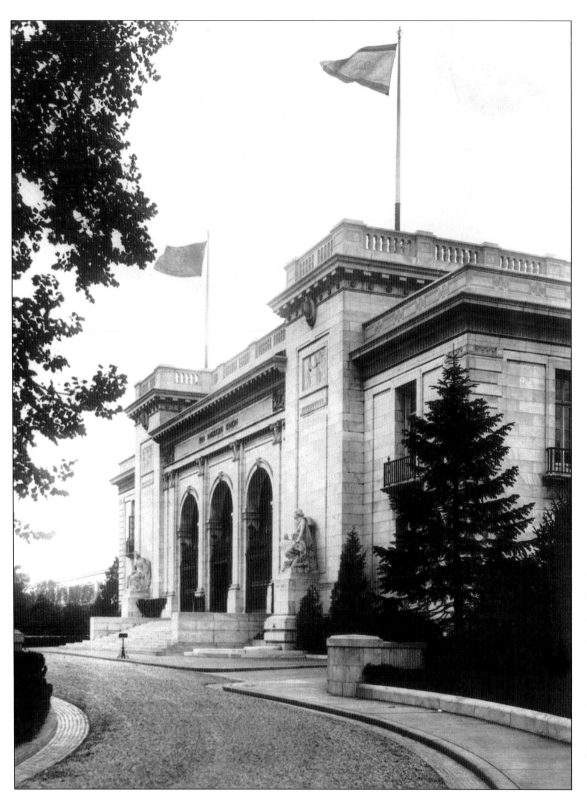

The headquarters of the Pan American Union, later the Organization of American States, was built at 17th Street and Constitution Avenue, NW, on the site of the Burnes House, one of the earliest houses in what would become the District of Columbia. Located adjacent to the White House South Lawn and at the very geographical center of the District, the Burnes House was built around 1750 by David Burnes, who died in 1799 after marketing many parcels of land in the immediate vicinity. An attempt at preservation was made by his sole daughter and her husband, who had built the adjacent Van Ness Mansion in 1816, but the Burnes House was demolished in 1894.

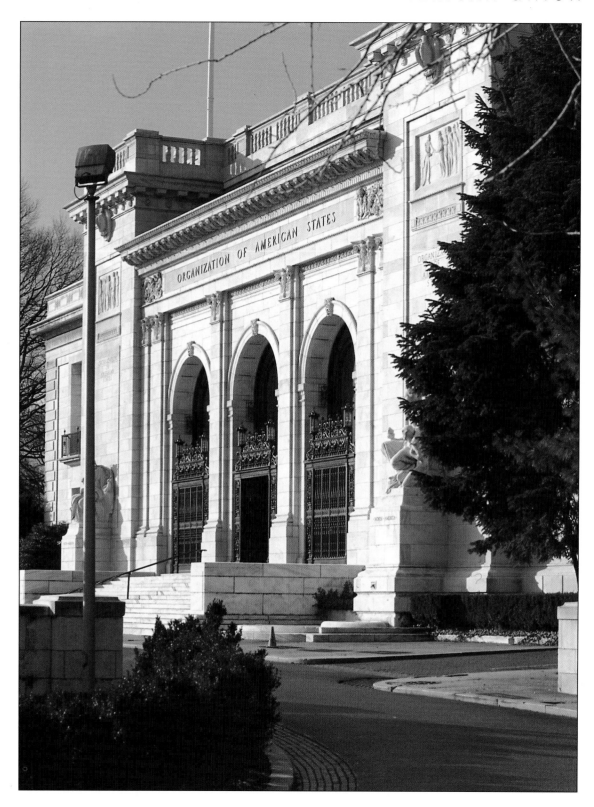

The property was sold to the government in 1907 after being used for everything from a beer garden to an athletic club to a street cleaners' headquarters. Andrew Carnegie donated $900,000 of the $1.1 million cost of the new building. The Pan American Union, formed in 1890, evolved into the present O.A.S. in 1948. It is a regional coalition of primarily Latin American and Caribbean nations, generally diplomatic and ceremonial in function, that works with the United Nations.

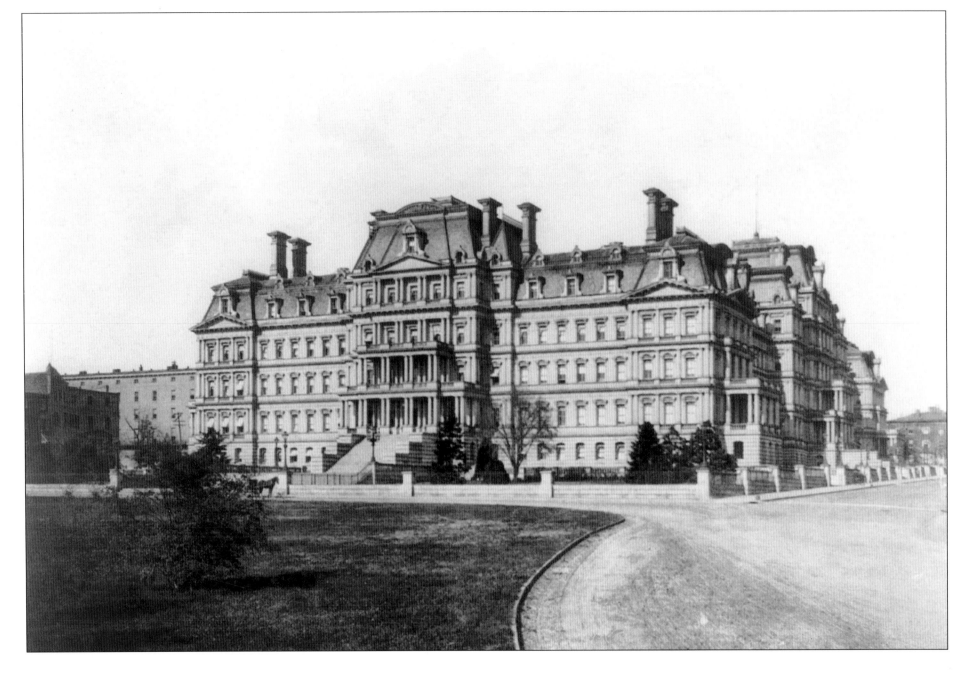

The old Department of War/State/Navy Building, arguably the most grandiose and ostentatious building in Washington, sits to the immediate west of the White House. Commissioned by Ulysses Grant and built between 1871 and 1888 on the site of the original 1800 War/State/Navy Building and the White House stables, this massive structure was for years the world's largest office building, with 566 rooms and about ten acres of floor space. This photograph of the building was taken in 1908.

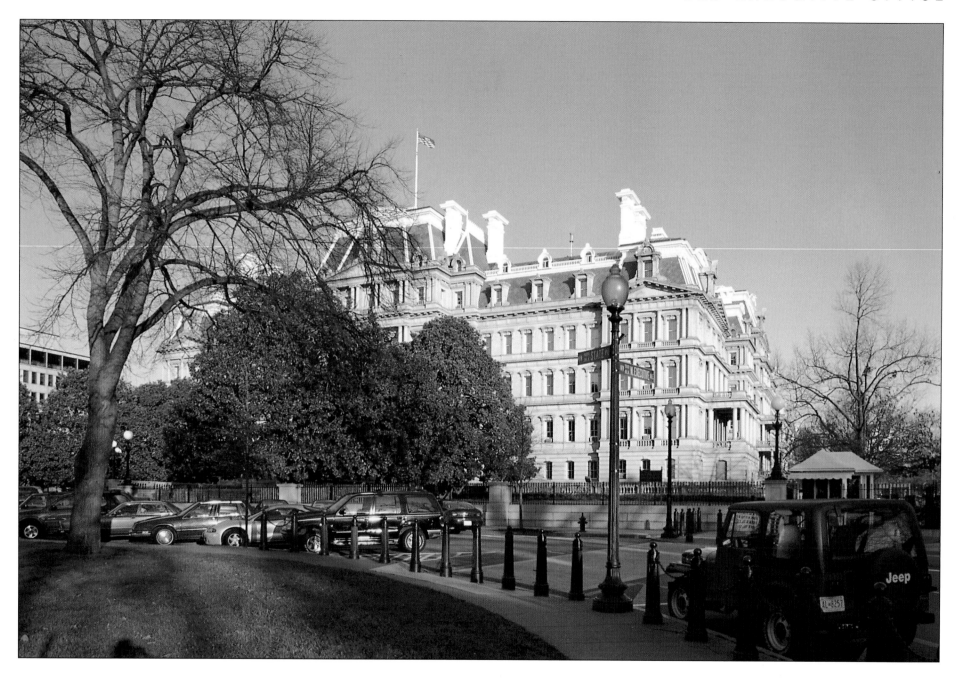

Patterned after French Empire architecture that clashed sharply with the neoclassical style of other Federal buildings in the city, it was generally regarded with scorn and disdain, and the architect of the exterior, Alfred B. Mullett, ended his life in litigation and suicide. The building is now popular with occupants, many of whom come from the executive branch of the government; Vice President Dan Quayle maintained his office here. It is said to still be the largest granite structure of any kind in the world.

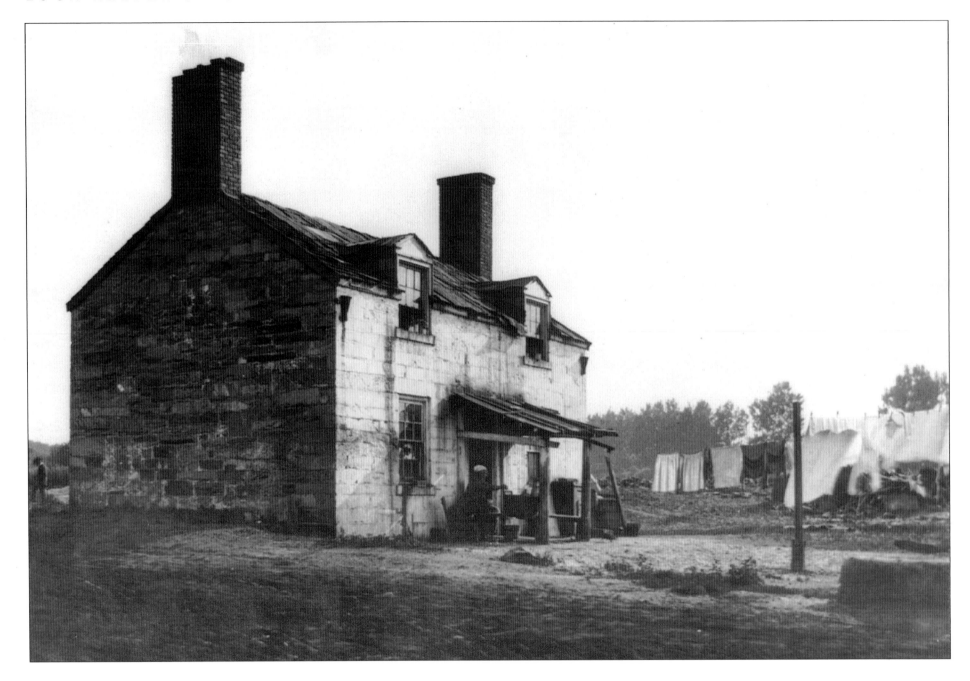

Unbelievably, this homely little house that sits at Constitution Avenue and 17th Street near the White House, looking for all the world like a grandiose public toilet, is one of the oldest surviving houses within Washington. Even more incredible, it once guarded the junction of what were at the time major national transportation arteries—the Potomac River and the Washington branch of the Chesapeake & Ohio Canal. Erected about 1835, it housed the keeper of the canal lock between the Washington Canal and the C&O branch, and sat on a narrow spit of land between the canal and the river. Later landfill would place this structure blocks from the Tidal Basin and nearly a half-mile from the Potomac proper.

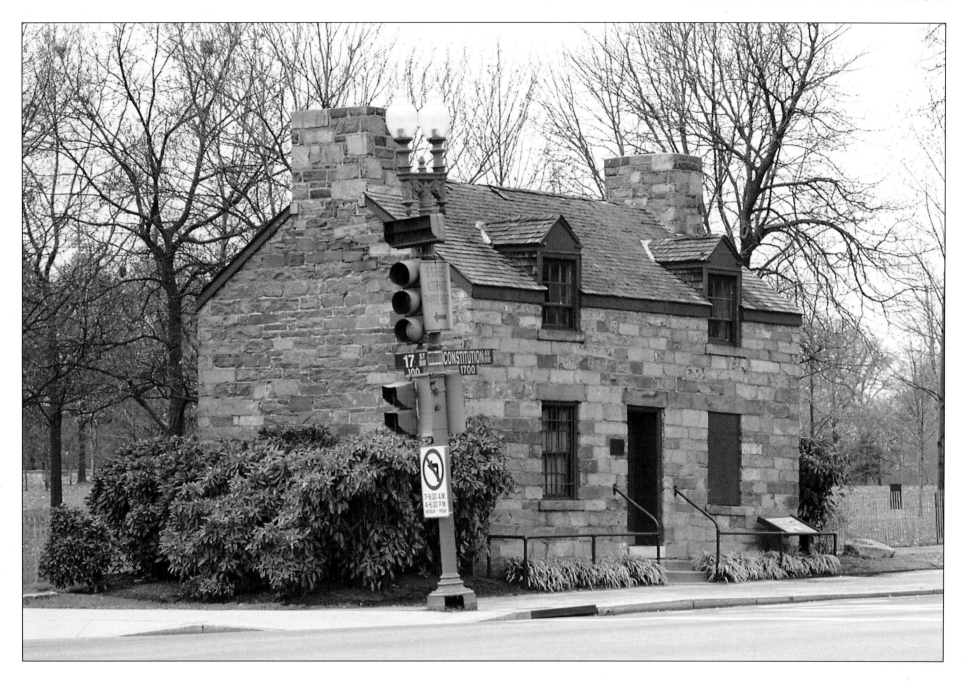

As the canal's use ended in the 1870s, the building saw a variety of
ignominious uses, including housing for squatters (as in the vintage photograph, which was taken in 1895). Today it sits empty but preserved by the
National Park Service, on a corner opposite from one of Charles Bulfinch's
guardhouses for the White House.

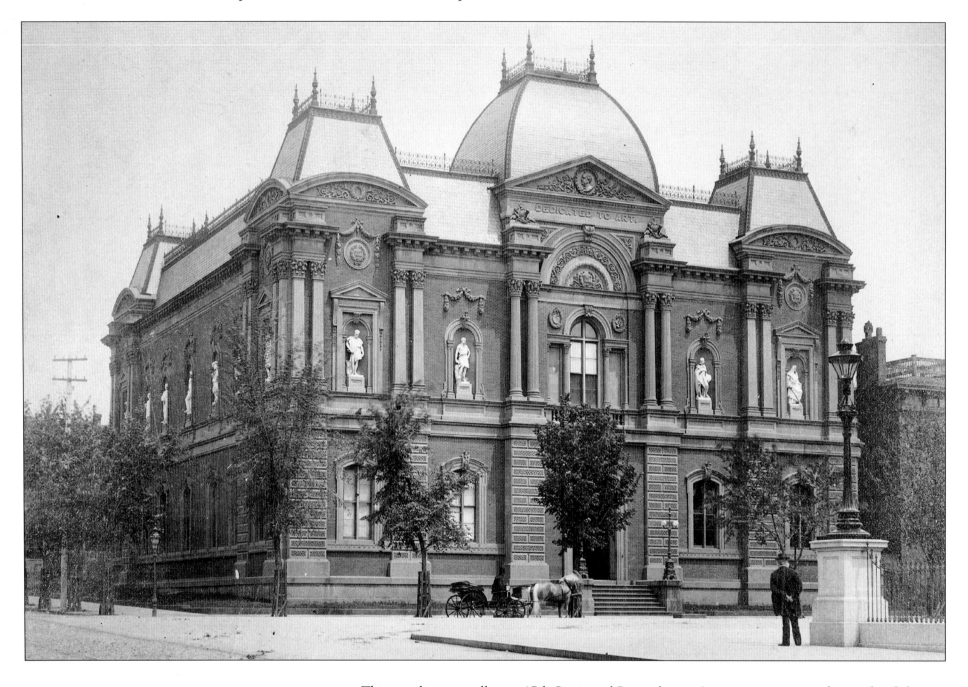

This grandiose art gallery at 17th Street and Pennsylvania Avenue was given to the city by philanthropist William Wilson Corcoran, a member of the Corcoran & Riggs firm that eventually grew into the local Riggs National Bank chain. Designed by James Renwick, Jr., construction on the building began in 1859, five years after Corcoran's retirement, and was completed as the Corcoran Gallery in 1871. The unfinished building was seized by the U.S. Government for office space during the Civil War; Corcoran's board of trustees sued for back rent and eventually collected $125,000.

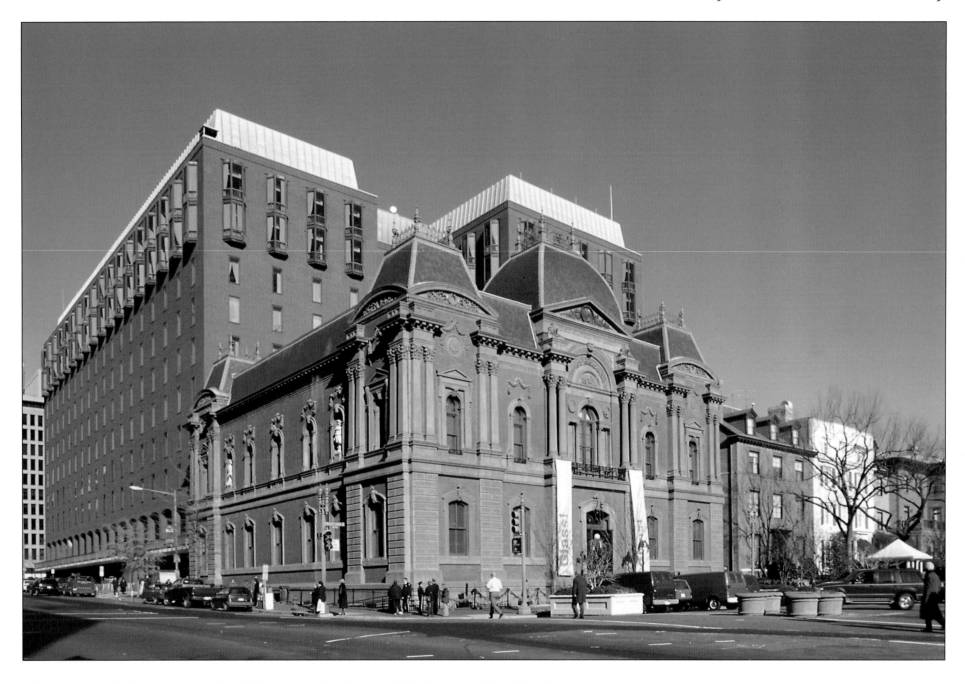

The Corcoran Gallery was moved in 1897 to a new building at 17th Street and New York Avenue, NW. The original gallery, now known as the Renwick Gallery and part of the Smithsonian's extensive complex, is used to display exhibitions of American craft art. The Grand Salon inside has been restored in the style of the late 19th century.

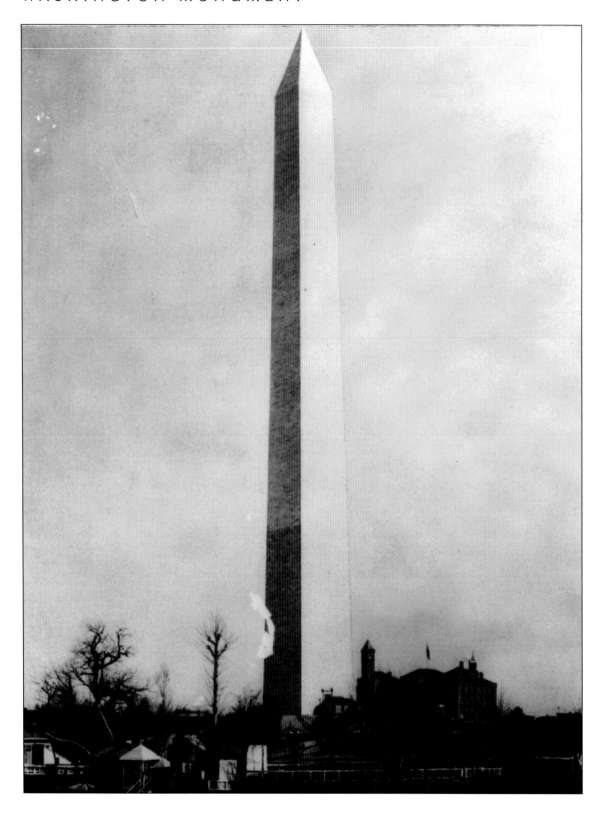

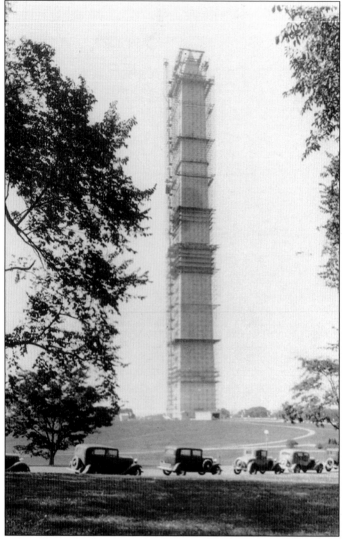

Construction on the memorial to the nation's first president was begun in 1848, but funding by public contribution ran out in 1853, and it stood uncompleted at 152 feet for nearly 25 years. The Federal government later approved funds to complete the structure and it was finished in December 1884, to a design radically simplified from Robert Mills' original colonnaded temple. Close examination will reveal a slight change in stone color at the 152-foot level, where Massachusetts marble was substituted for the earlier Maryland marble. The smaller photograph above shows a cleaning project in 1934–35, which took a matter of weeks.

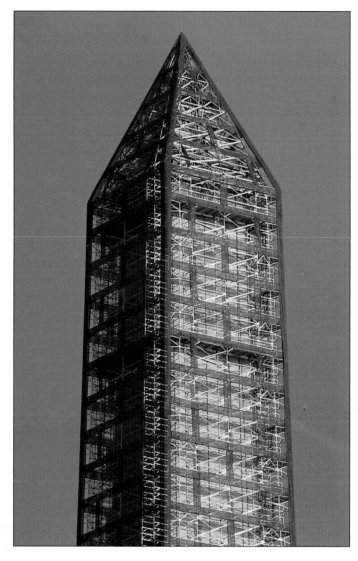

The end of the 20th century brought a dramatic change to one of the most recognizable monuments in the world as scaffolding and shrouding was erected for cleaning and repairing the 555-foot structure. The shrouding of the monument for over a year was originally greeted with aversion, but ironically, as the scaffolding was being disassembled at press time, efforts were being made to preserve and re-erect the scaffolding and its sympathetic shrouding elsewhere!

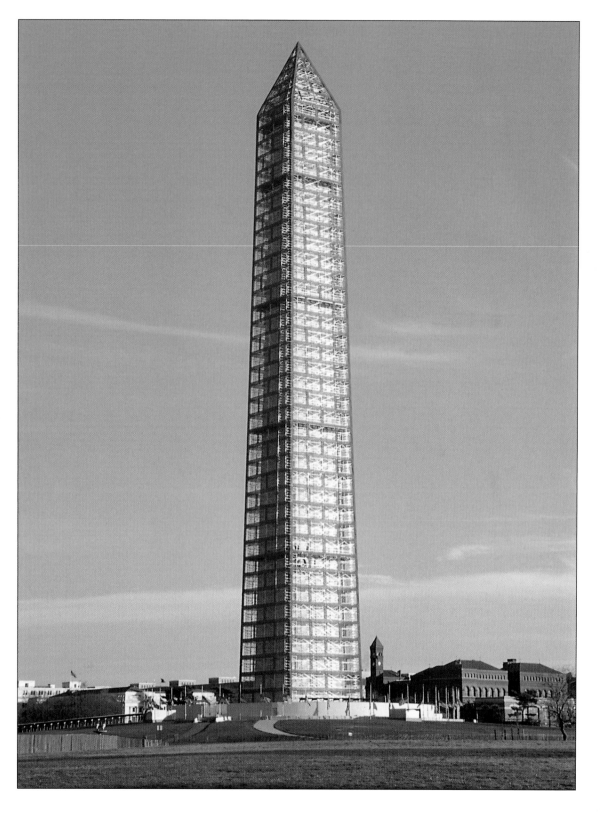

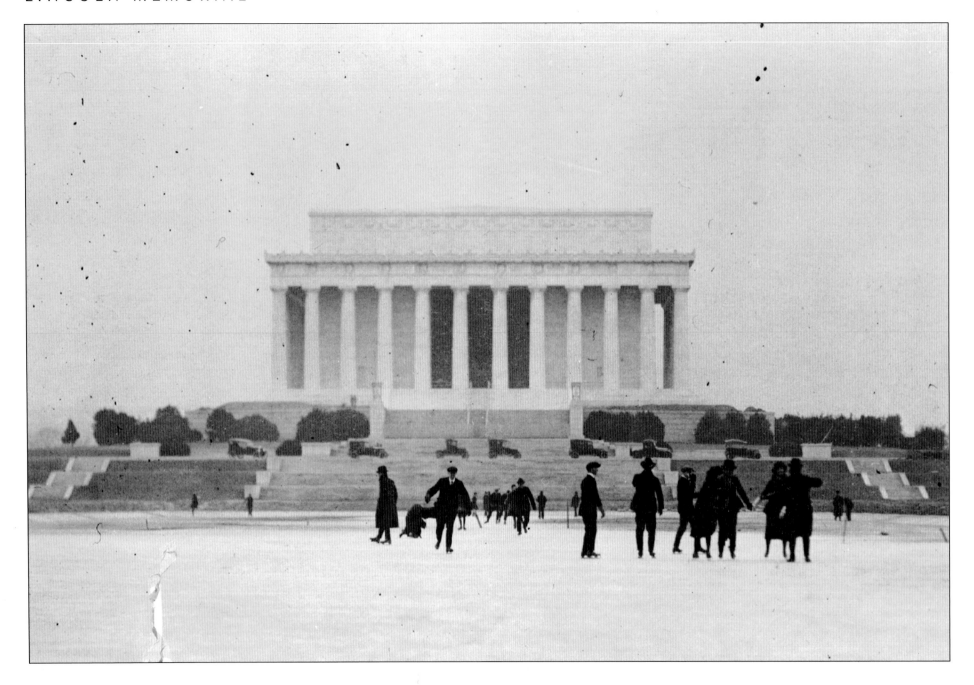

The Lincoln Memorial was constructed between 1914 and 1921 to a design (modeled after a Greek temple) by Henry Bacon, and dedicated in 1922. The memorial has 36 Doric columns representing the 36 states of the Union at the time of Lincoln's death, and is centered by the famous heroic statue of Lincoln by Daniel Chester French.

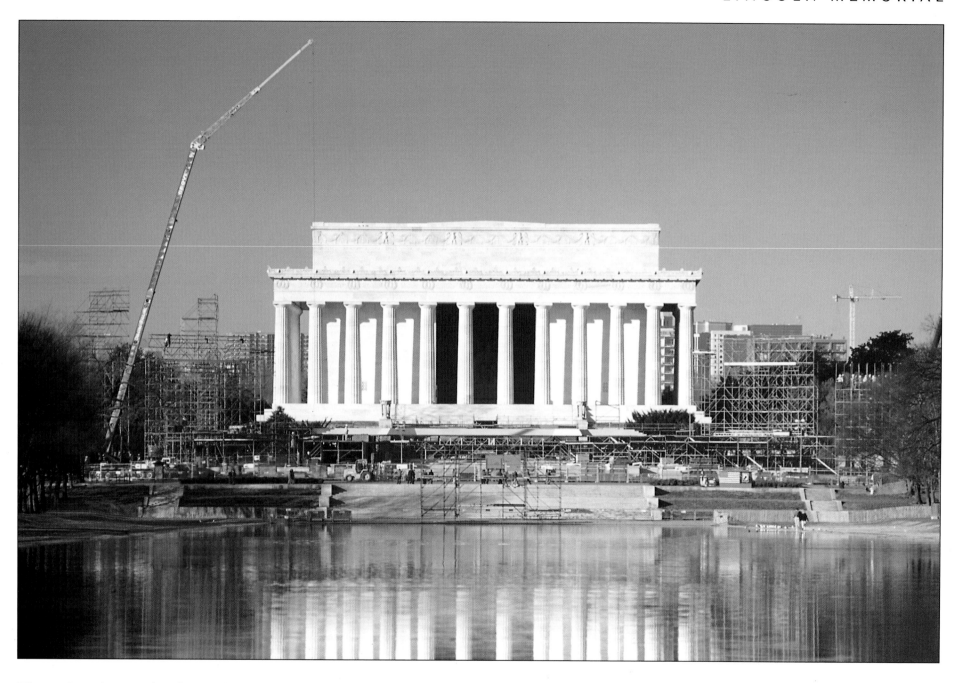

The modern photograph, taken at the end of 1999, shows the monument surrounded by staging and scaffolding being erected for the New Year 2000 celebrations about to occur weeks later. The Reflecting Pool, 2,000 feet long, was inspired by similar pools at the Taj Mahal and Versailles, and stretches from the Lincoln Memorial to the Rainbow Pool next to the Washington Monument.

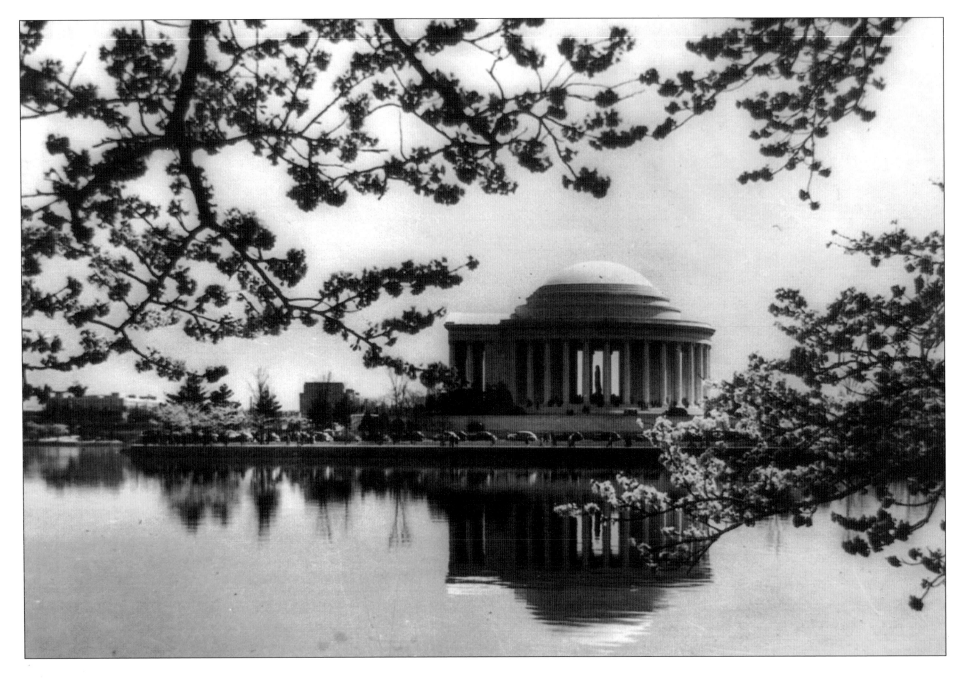

The memorial to Thomas Jefferson on the Tidal Basin was authorized by Congress, built in 1938–42, and dedicated in 1943. Designed by John Russell Pope (who also did the National Gallery of Art and the National Archives), the white marble structure features a 19-foot-tall bronze statue of the third president (by sculptor Rudolph Evans) surrounded by 26 columns.

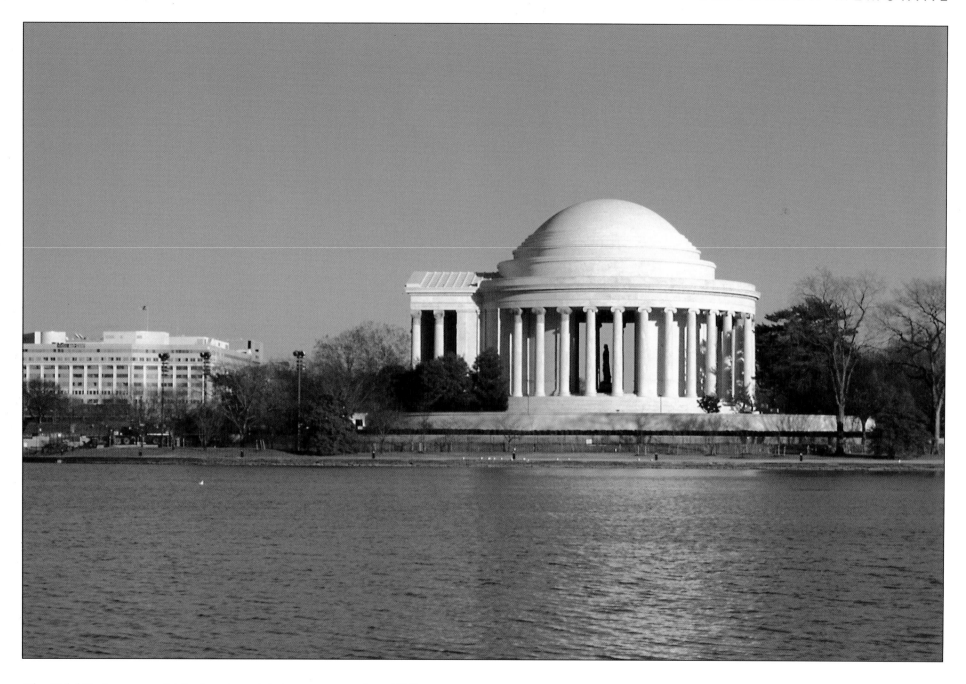

The Tidal Basin, upon which the memorial sits, was created in 1882 to trap overflow water from the Potomac River and drain it into the Washington Channel. It is ringed with cherry trees given by the city of Tokyo to the city of Washington. The first shipment arrived in 1912. The annual springtime blooming of these trees is now an internationally-renowned tourist attraction.

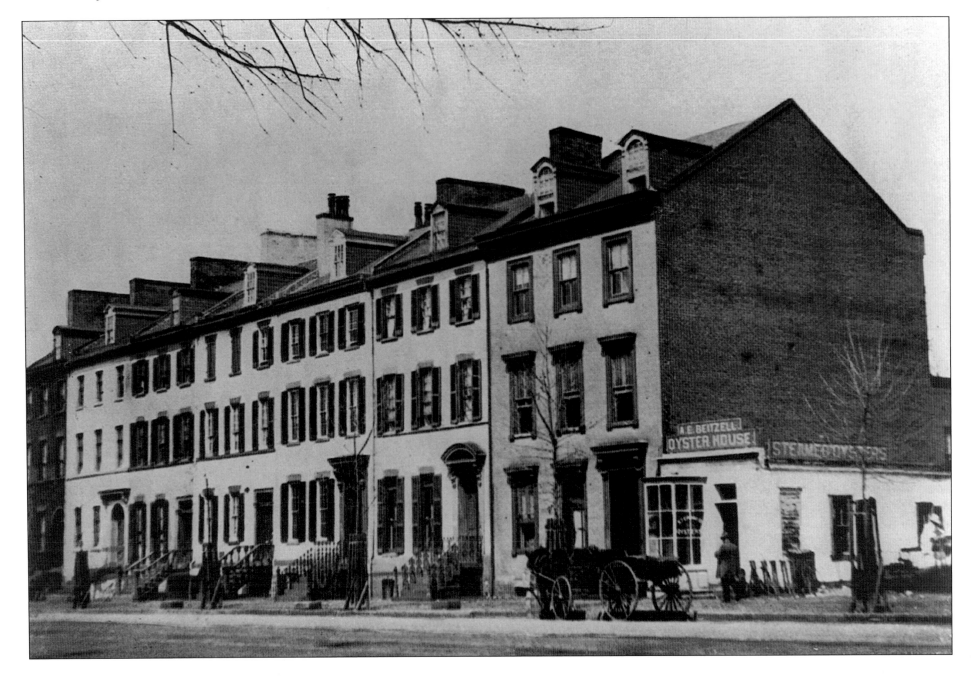

Occupying the north side of the 2000 Block of Pennsylvania Avenue, NW, the Six Buildings (seen as seven in this photo) were built about 1800 by Isaac Pollock, an important early investor in the city who (like many early investors) lost almost all his money on property ventures gone sour. For a period, the buildings housed the U.S. Department of State.

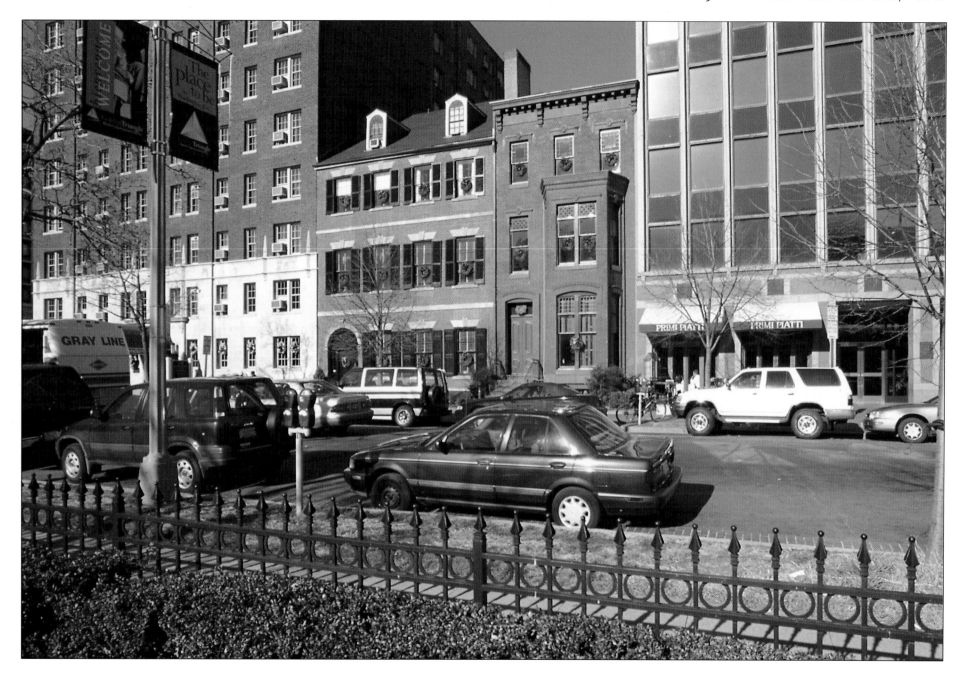

In 1999, one of the buildings, privately owned and actually a consolidation of parts of two of the older buildings, survives, sandwiched between the Hotel Lombardi and a newer brick residence and office building.

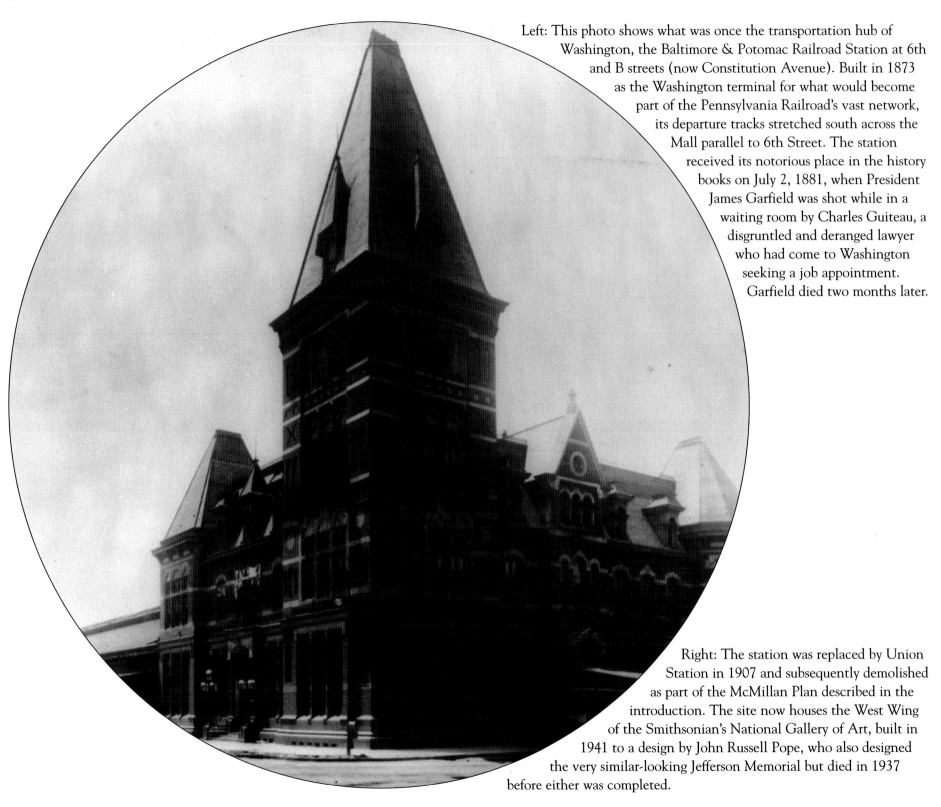

Left: This photo shows what was once the transportation hub of Washington, the Baltimore & Potomac Railroad Station at 6th and B streets (now Constitution Avenue). Built in 1873 as the Washington terminal for what would become part of the Pennsylvania Railroad's vast network, its departure tracks stretched south across the Mall parallel to 6th Street. The station received its notorious place in the history books on July 2, 1881, when President James Garfield was shot while in a waiting room by Charles Guiteau, a disgruntled and deranged lawyer who had come to Washington seeking a job appointment. Garfield died two months later.

Right: The station was replaced by Union Station in 1907 and subsequently demolished as part of the McMillan Plan described in the introduction. The site now houses the West Wing of the Smithsonian's National Gallery of Art, built in 1941 to a design by John Russell Pope, who also designed the very similar-looking Jefferson Memorial but died in 1937 before either was completed.

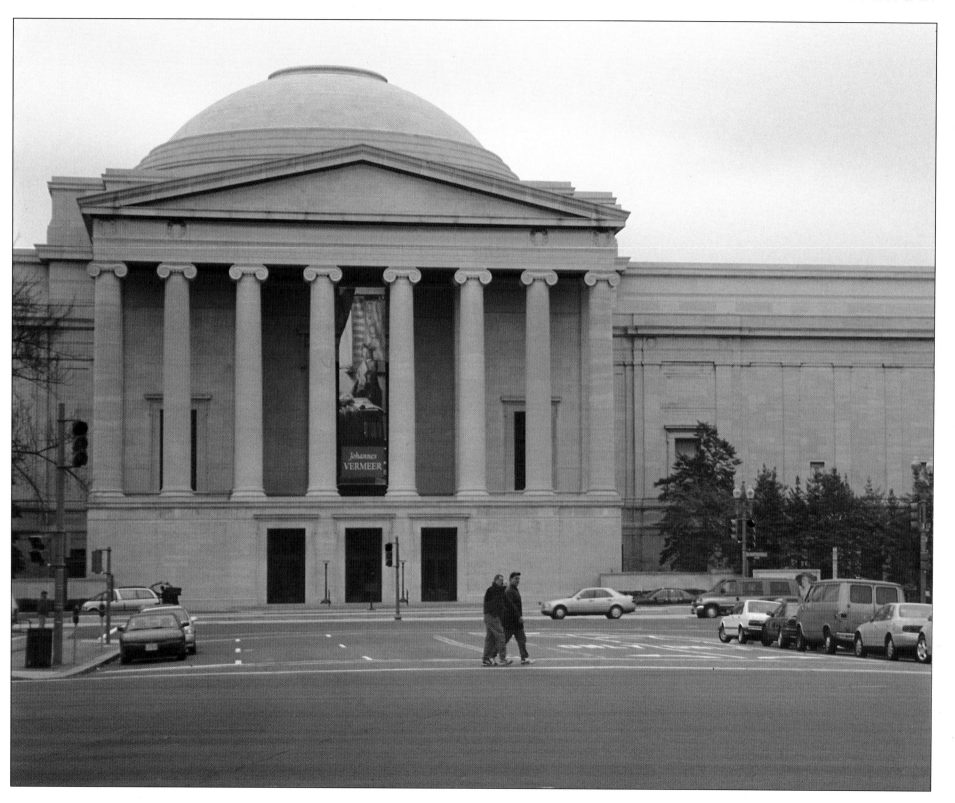

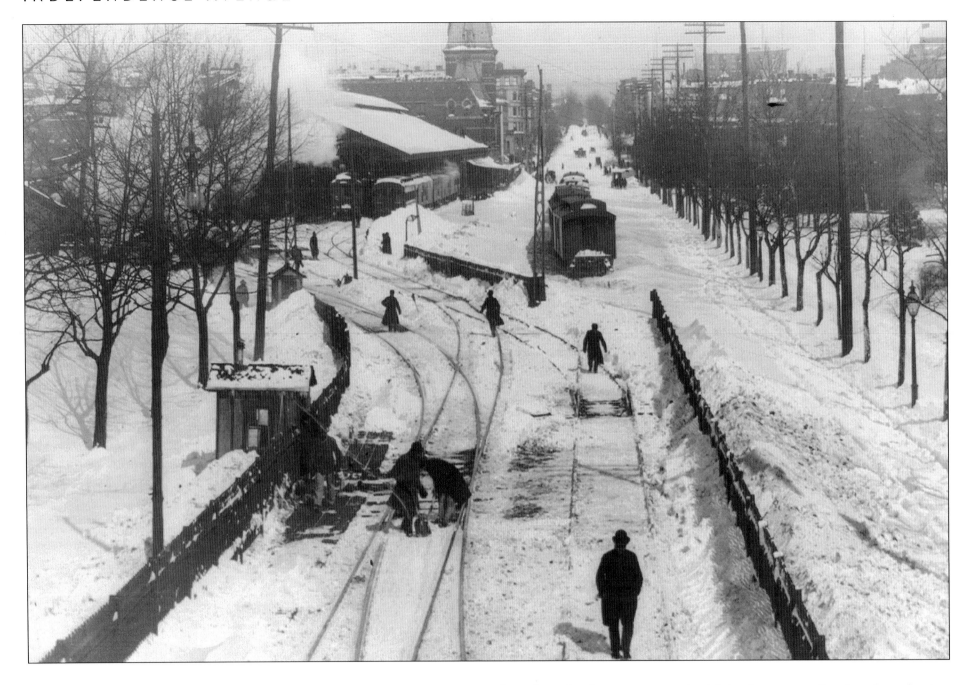

In perhaps the sharpest contrast in this book, we see railroad workers clearing snow from the tracks leading to the trainshed of the Baltimore & Potomac R.R. Station after the blizzard of 1893, as viewed from a bridge over the tracks in the vicinity of present-day Independence Avenue.

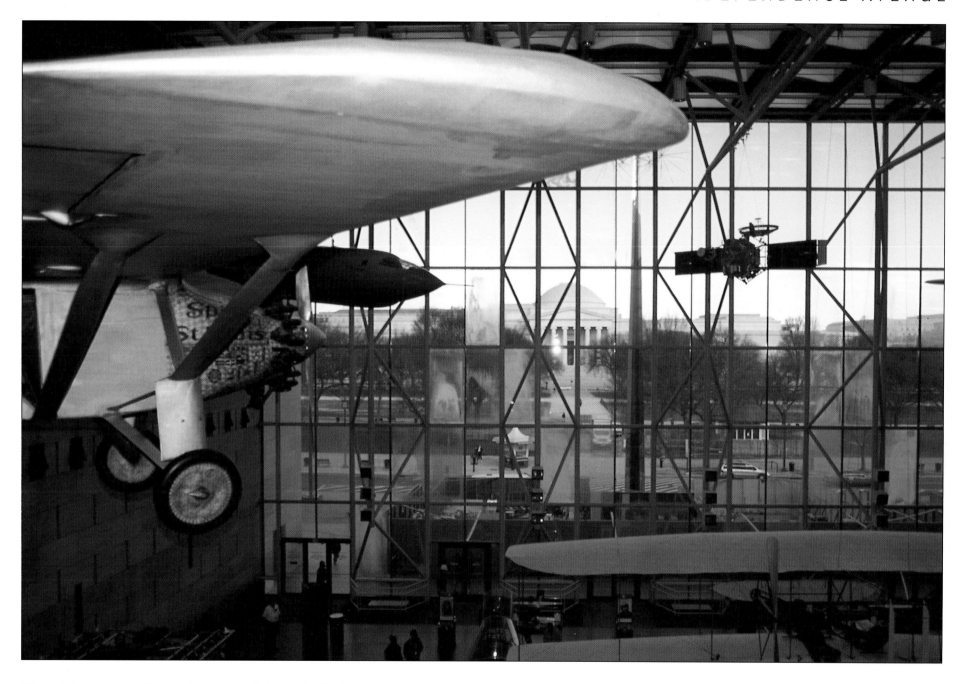

The modern view looks out the main exhibition hall of the Smithsonian's National Air & Space Museum (opened in 1976), underneath the wing of Charles Lindbergh's *Spirit of St. Louis*, over a Wright Brothers' plane, and across a now-open mall toward the National Gallery of Art.

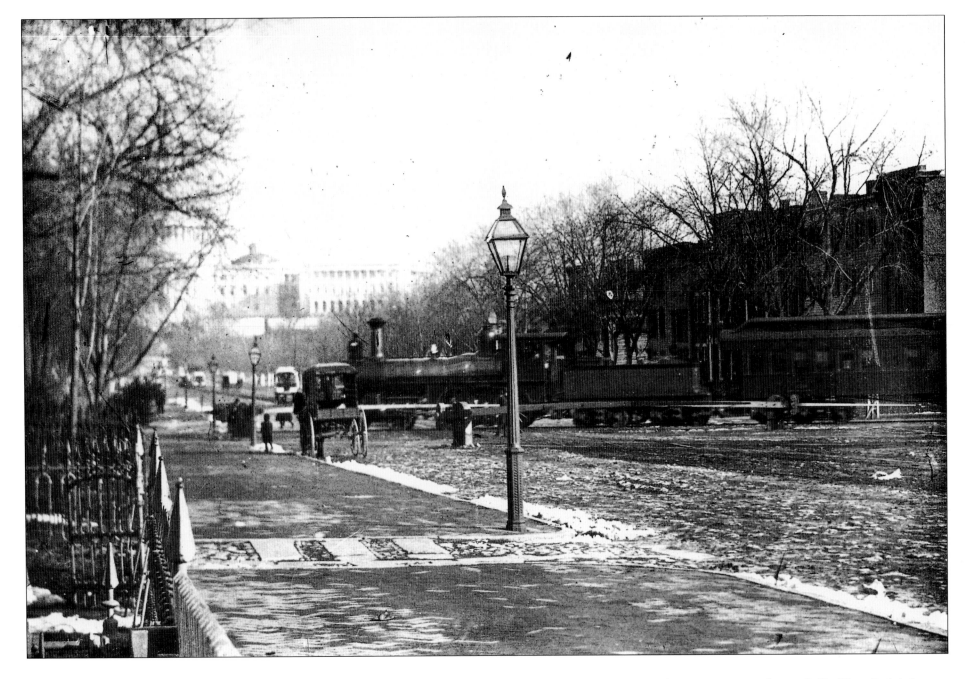

In this view from approximately 1880, a Pennsylvania R.R. Class D 4-4-0 locomotive crosses Maryland Avenue between 6th and 7th streets on its final approach to the Baltimore and Potomac depot. Not only did P.R.R. trains cross the heart of the Mall until 1907, but Maryland Avenue was once the route for much of the nation's rail traffic between the North and the South before and after the Civil War. Note the gas lamps and the long crossing gates.

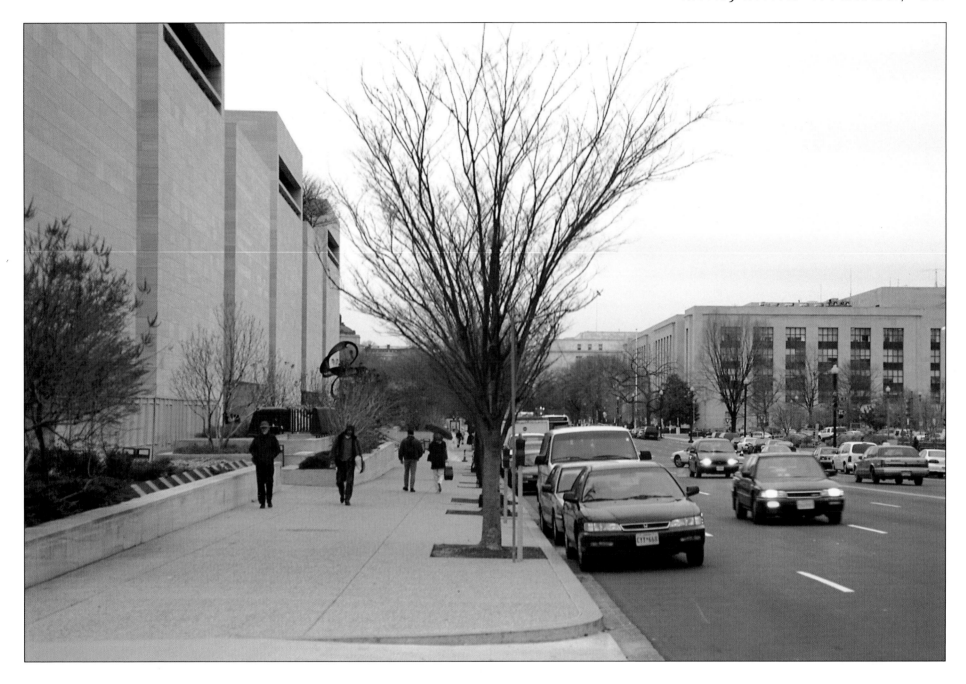

The modern view through a realigned intersection is partially blocked by the south wall of the National Air and Space Museum to the left; the Department of Health & Human Services and the Rayburn Office Building of the House of Representatives can be seen further up Independence Avenue.

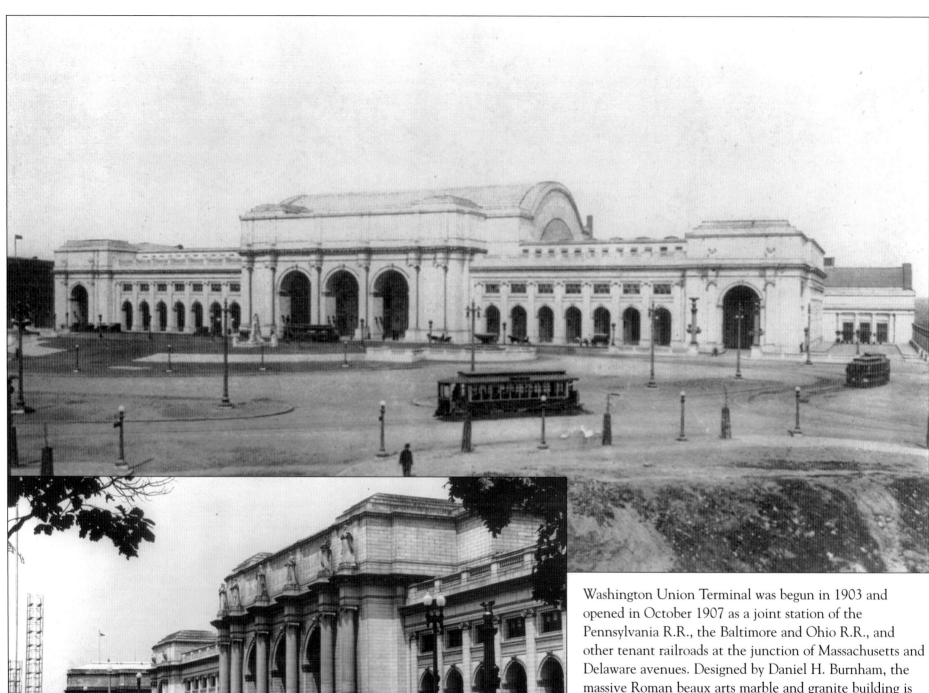

Washington Union Terminal was begun in 1903 and opened in October 1907 as a joint station of the Pennsylvania R.R., the Baltimore and Ohio R.R., and other tenant railroads at the junction of Massachusetts and Delaware avenues. Designed by Daniel H. Burnham, the massive Roman beaux arts marble and granite building is marginally larger than the Capitol itself, and includes a concourse of 760 by 130 feet, said to be the largest room of any kind in the world when built.

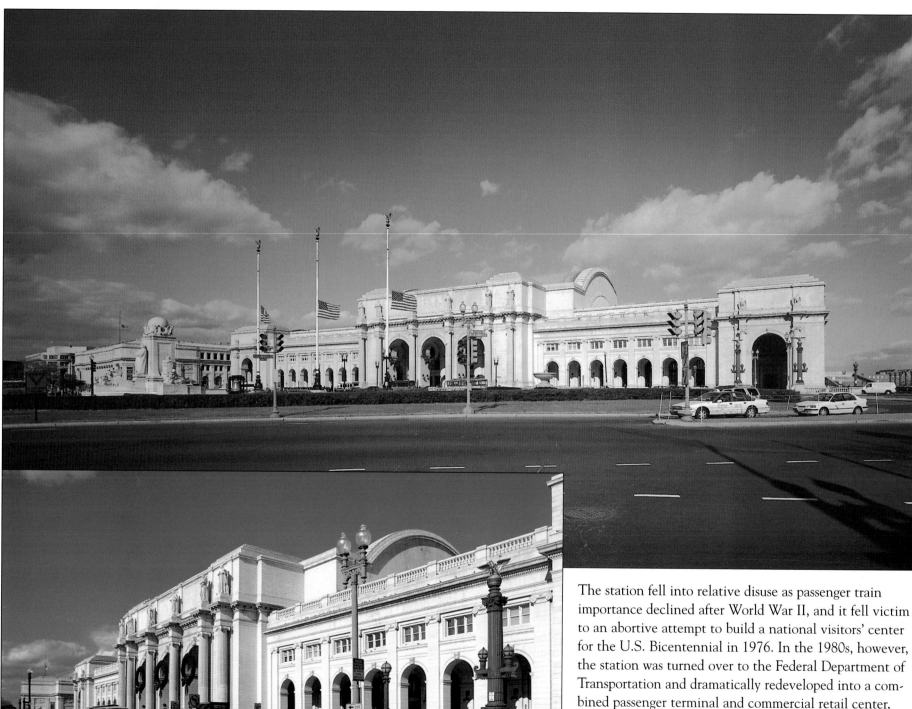

The station fell into relative disuse as passenger train importance declined after World War II, and it fell victim to an abortive attempt to build a national visitors' center for the U.S. Bicentennial in 1976. In the 1980s, however, the station was turned over to the Federal Department of Transportation and dramatically redeveloped into a combined passenger terminal and commercial retail center, with enormous success. It is now said that it rivals the National Air & Space Museum as the most-visited Washington attraction. The rail station still sees an average of nearly 100 trains a day.

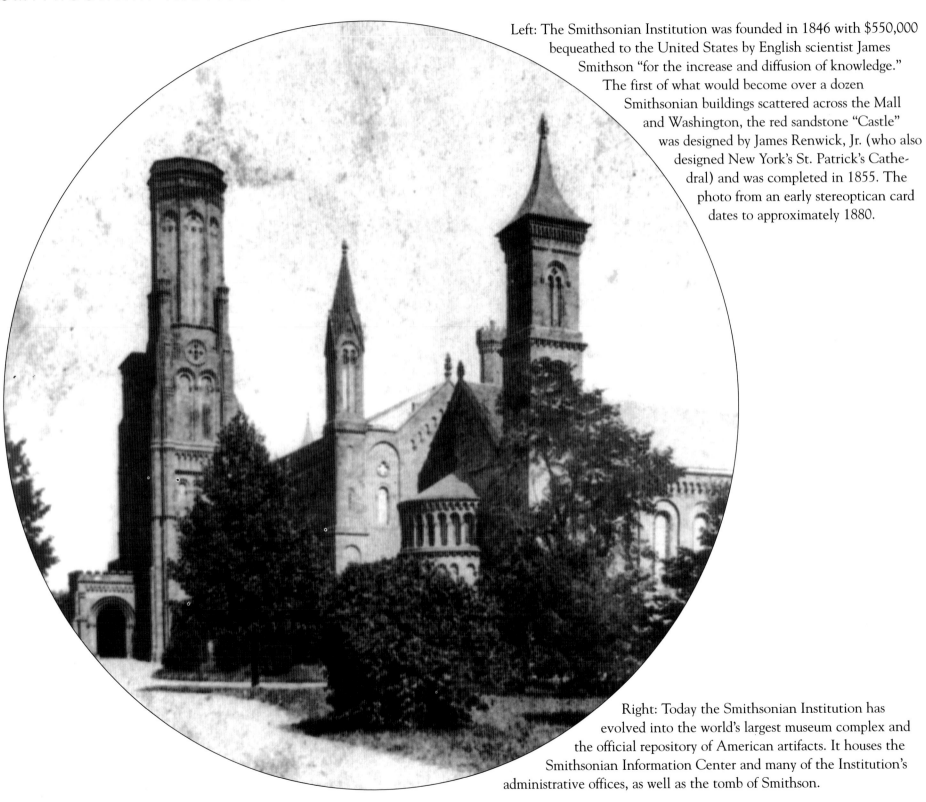

Left: The Smithsonian Institution was founded in 1846 with $550,000 bequeathed to the United States by English scientist James Smithson "for the increase and diffusion of knowledge." The first of what would become over a dozen Smithsonian buildings scattered across the Mall and Washington, the red sandstone "Castle" was designed by James Renwick, Jr. (who also designed New York's St. Patrick's Cathedral) and was completed in 1855. The photo from an early stereoptican card dates to approximately 1880.

Right: Today the Smithsonian Institution has evolved into the world's largest museum complex and the official repository of American artifacts. It houses the Smithsonian Information Center and many of the Institution's administrative offices, as well as the tomb of Smithson.

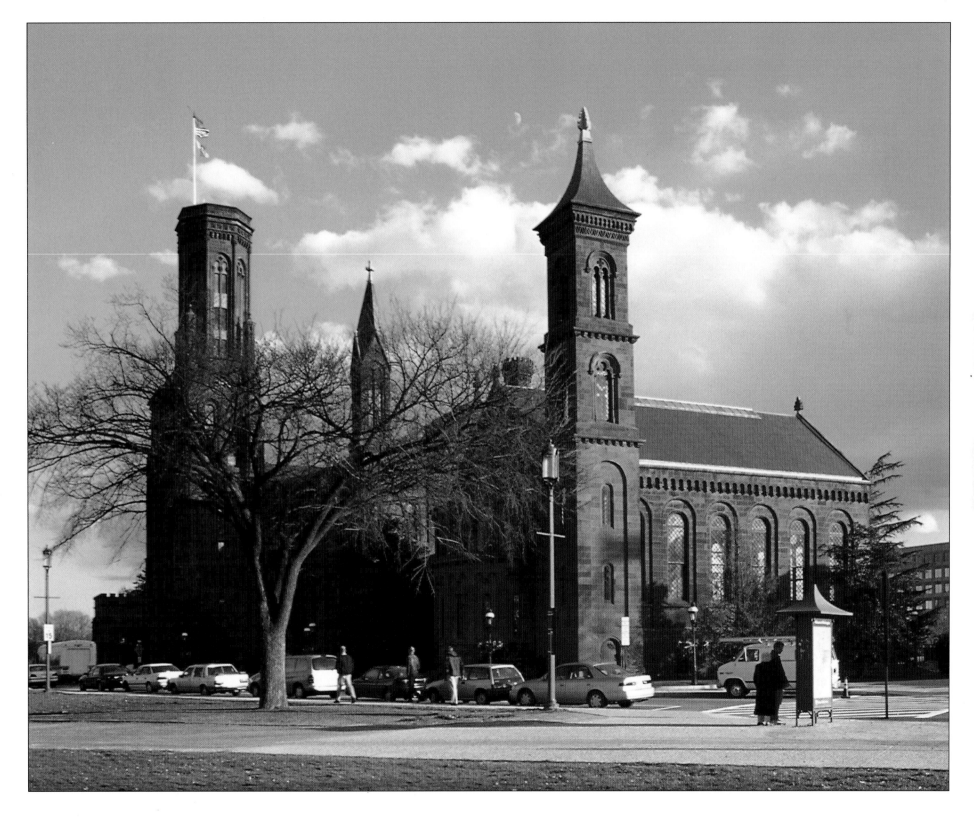

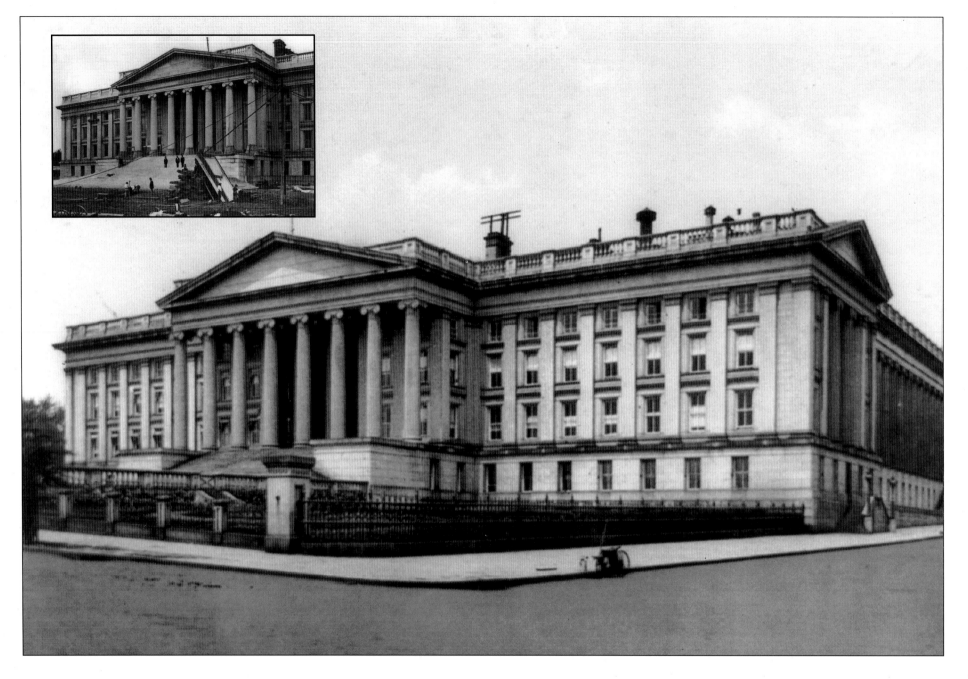

The General Post Office, the U.S. Patent Office, and the U.S. Treasury were all principally designed (in part as permanent fireproof buildings) by Robert Mills, who was appointed Federal Architect of Public Buildings by President Andrew Jackson in 1836. That same year construction began on the Treasury Building on a site personally selected by Jackson in the first radical departure from the city plan drafted by L'Enfant. The building features 74 granite columns, all boated in from Maine quarries. The inset photo shows the building in 1867, two years before its completion.

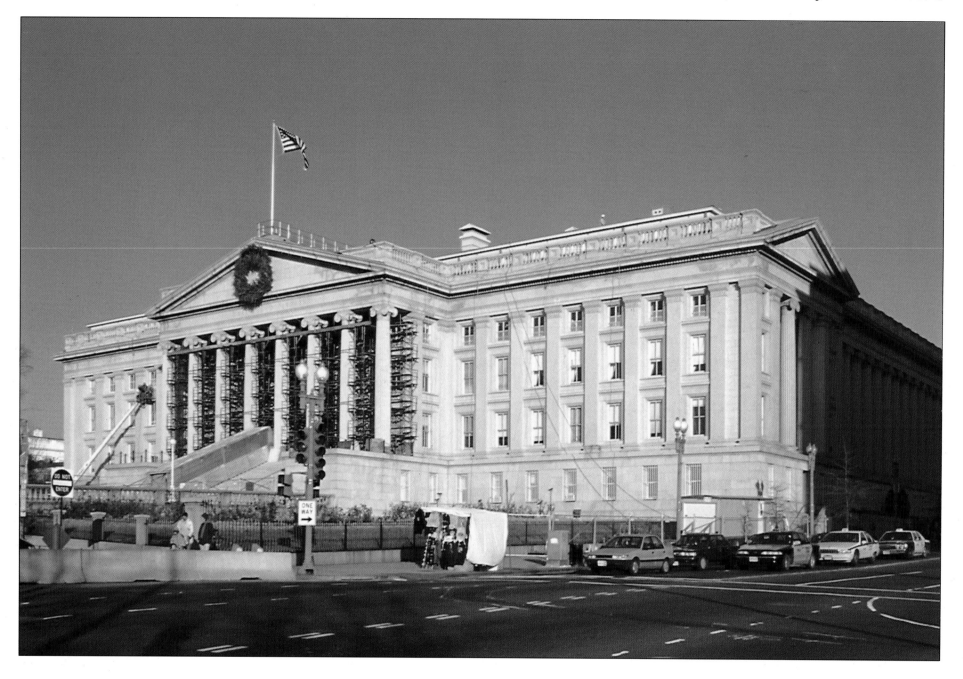

The southern façade features a statue of Alexander Hamilton, the first Treasury Secretary. Featured on the reverse of every $10 bill (along with four vintage automobiles), the building continues to house the Treasury Department today. The original sandstone colonnades, however, were replaced with granite in 1907.

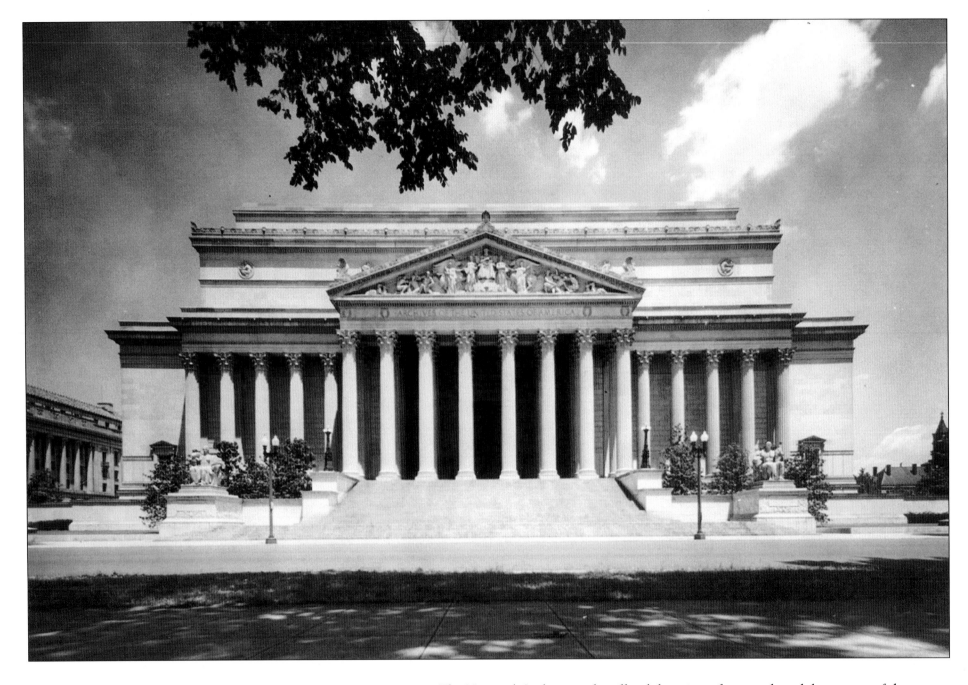

The National Archives is the official depository for records and documents of the federal government. In 1926, after decades of records being lost to haphazard accounting and storage, Congress arranged for the construction of a central repository where records could be assembled, stored, and preserved. In 1934 the National Archives was organized, to be administered by a central archivist, and the building was completed on the site of the former Central Market.

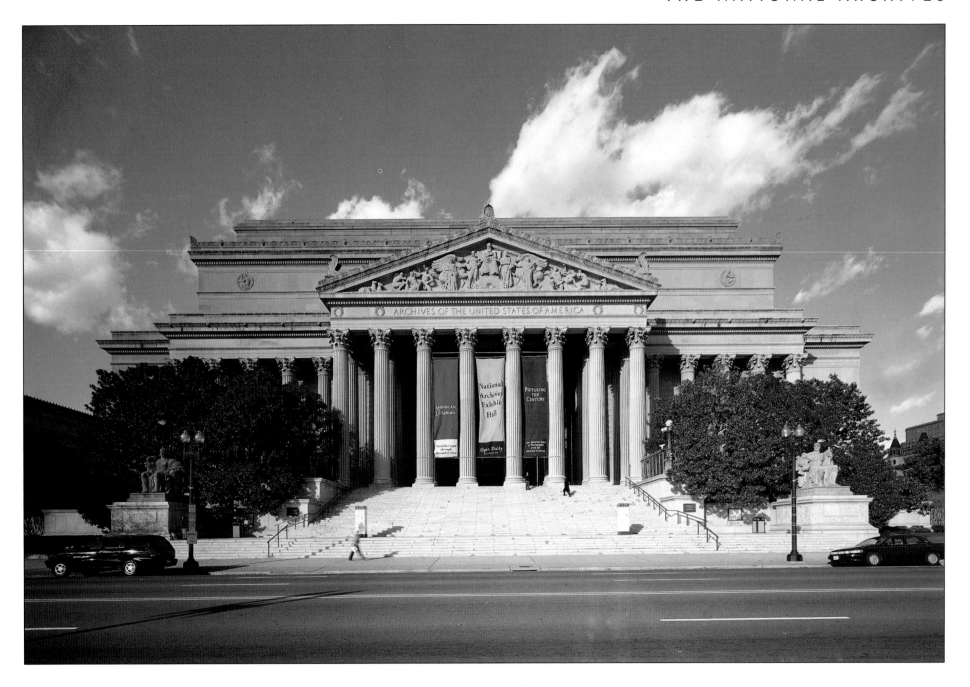

The building is perhaps best known among tourists as the building housing the original copies of the Declaration of Independence, Constitution, and Bill of Rights. Like many buildings housing Federal agencies in Washington, the Archive's duties are now supplemented by additional facilities in suburban Maryland.

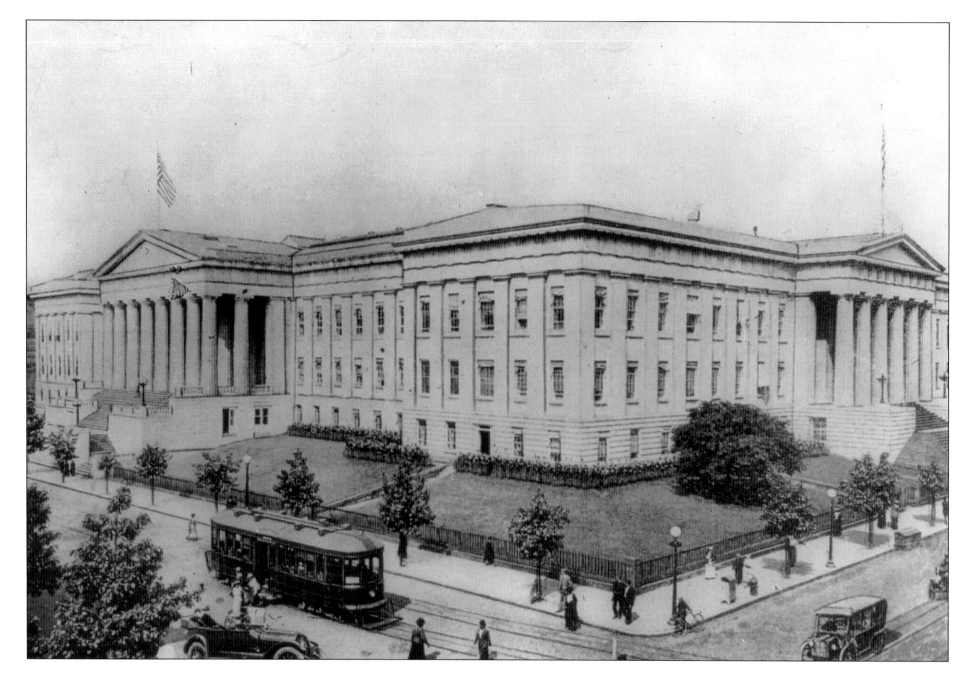

The headquarters of invention registration in the United States, construction on the Patent Office was begun in 1836 and completed in 1867. During the Civil War the uncompleted building was used as a hospital. Burned in 1877, it was rebuilt in the 1880's by noted architect Adolph Cluss. After its renovation, part of the building housed a small museum of patent models of many important American inventions. The actual offices of the Patent Office were moved in 1932, and the building was then occupied by the Civil Service Commission until 1952.

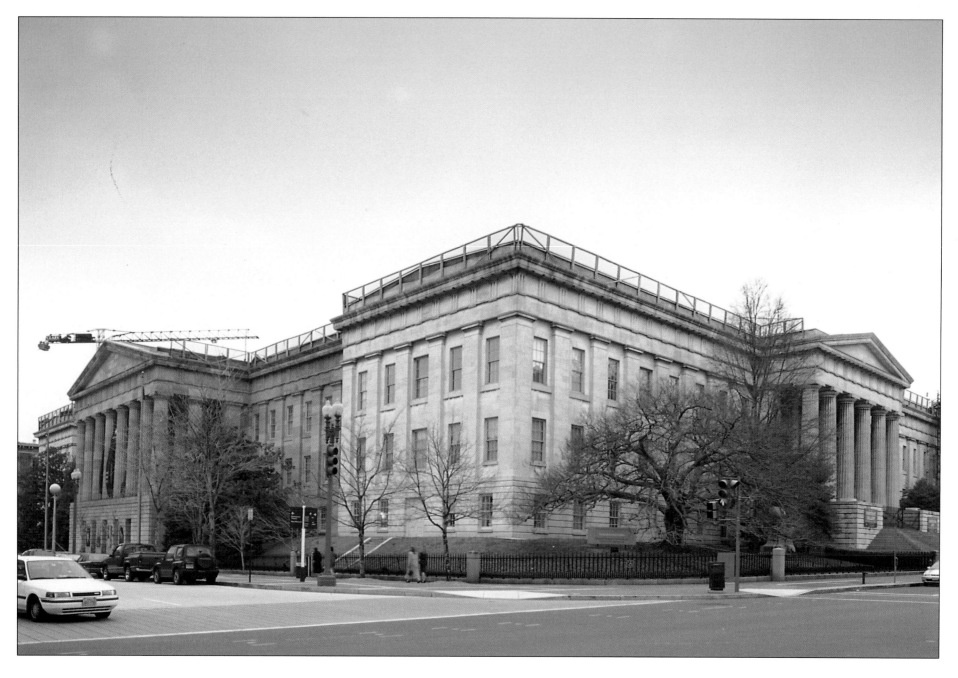

Slated for demolition, the Patent Office was spared primarily through the efforts of David Finley, the chairman of the Fine Arts Commission, and was transferred to the Smithsonian Institution and restored in 1968 as the headquarters of the National Museum of American Art and the National Portrait Gallery. In 2000, however, the building stood awaiting closure and a three-year renovation.

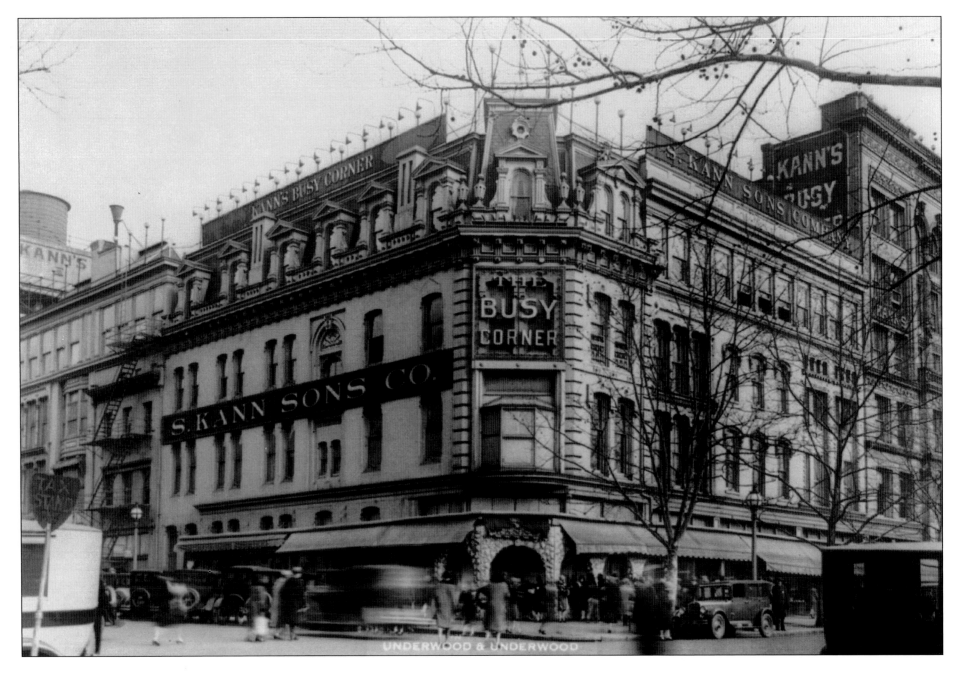

This 1920s view shows one part of the heart of the downtown shopping district, at Pennsylvania Avenue and 7th Street. S. Kann Sons department store was located in the building that originally housed the first clothing store operated by Isidore and Andrew Saks (later of Saks 5th Ave. fame), which later became the Boston Dry Goods store, which itself grew into the local Woodward & Lothrop chain.

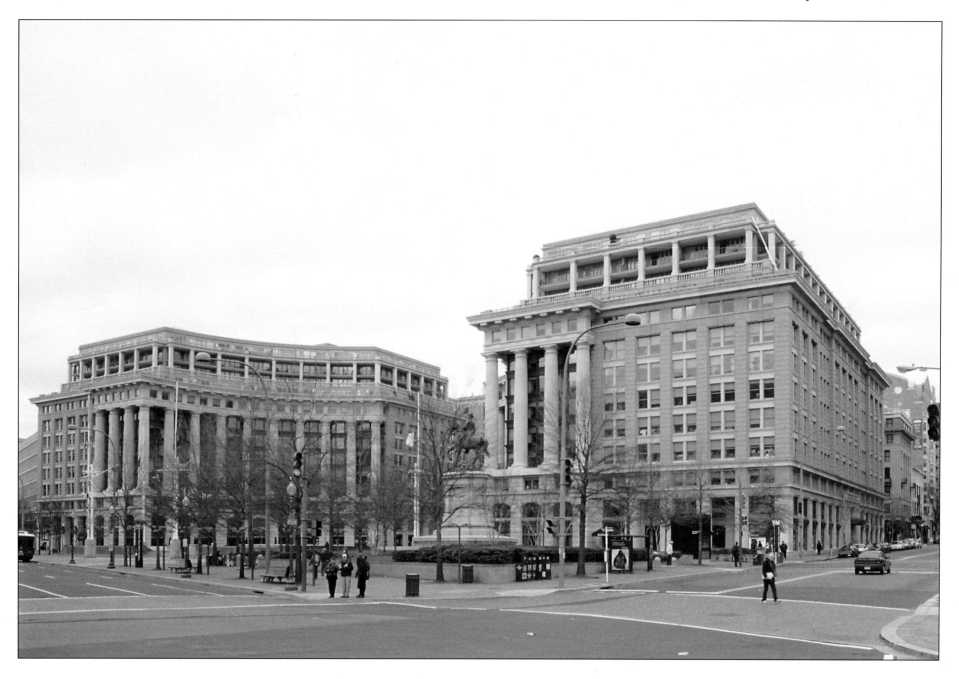

Kann's occupied the building from 1886 until the building's demolition in 1979 following a serious fire. The site is now the location of the U.S. Navy Memorial, dedicated in October 1987, which includes an amphitheater for performances by the Navy Band and other groups.

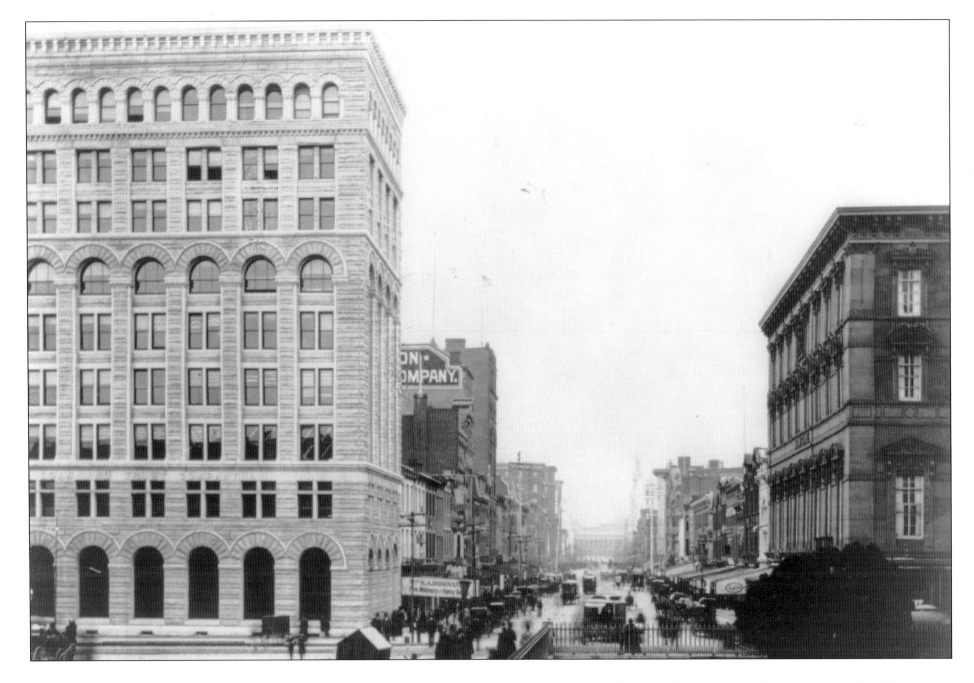

This view looking west from the steps of the Patent Office, taken around 1900, shows a rapidly developing commercial district downtown. To the left is the Washington Loan & Trust Co. Building, erected 1890, and later the Riggs National Bank WL&T Branch. Behind the bank can be seen the recently built National Union Insurance Co. building, with its sign at the top plainly visible. To the left at 901 F Street is the Masonic Hall, begun in 1868, which had shops on the ground floor and meeting rooms above.

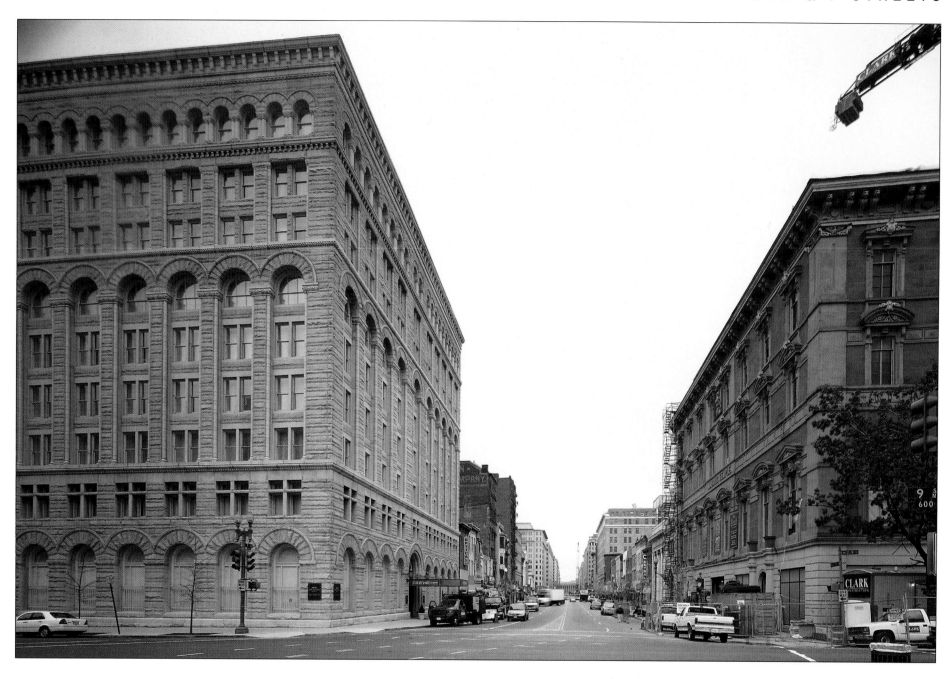

In the modern view, a hotel chain occupies the former WL&T Building; the signage for the insurance company is still faintly visible, and the Masonic Hall, vacant for over 20 years, was being redeveloped as commercial space as the Gallup Building. At the far end of F Street in both views can be seen the Treasury Building.

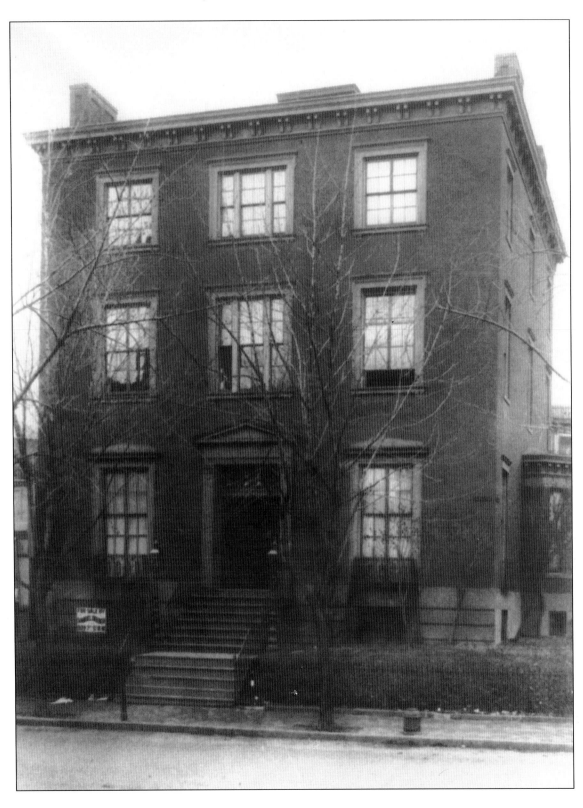

Left: This was the home of Salmon P. Chase, one of the lesser-remarked but important figures in American history. An active abolitionist and early member of the Republican Party, he was elected as governor of Ohio in 1855 and to the U.S. Senate in 1860, but was quickly tapped as Lincoln's Secretary of the Treasury, where he proposed and oversaw the formation of the national bank system. Lincoln appointed him to the Supreme Court in December 1864, where he oversaw many of the postwar Reconstruction cases and the impeachment of Andrew Johnson. The building at 6th and E streets, NW, was one of the buildings Chase occupied in Washington.

Right: Today, the national headquarters of the American Association of Retired Persons occupies the corner that once housed such a vigorous politician.

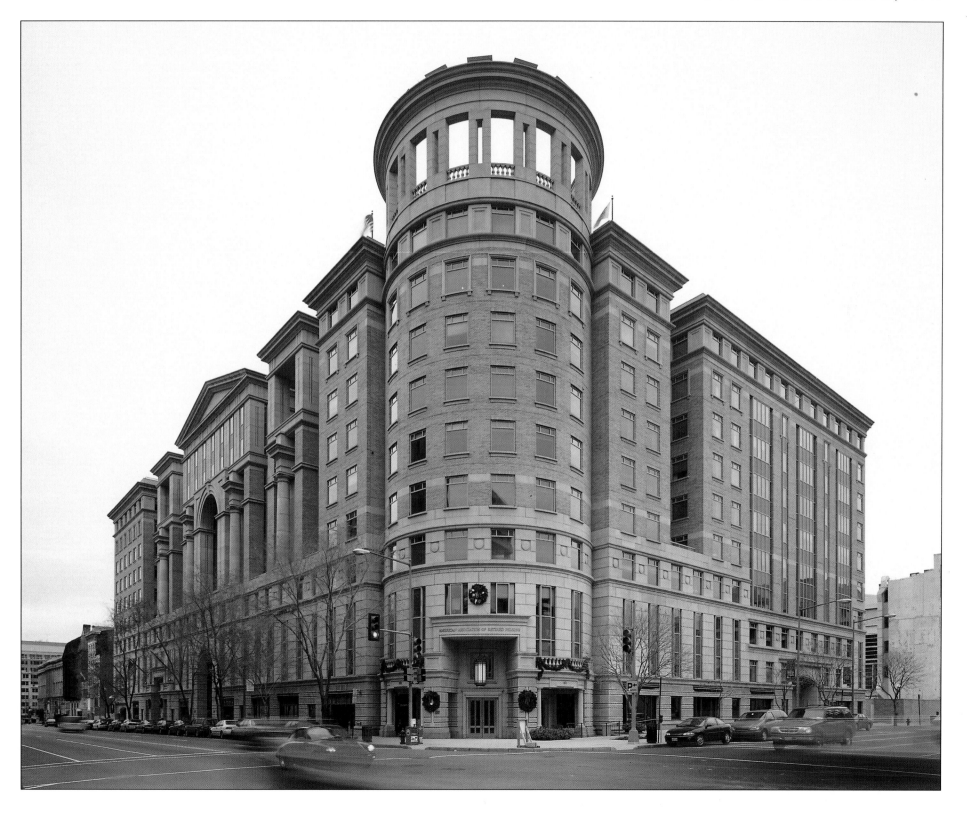

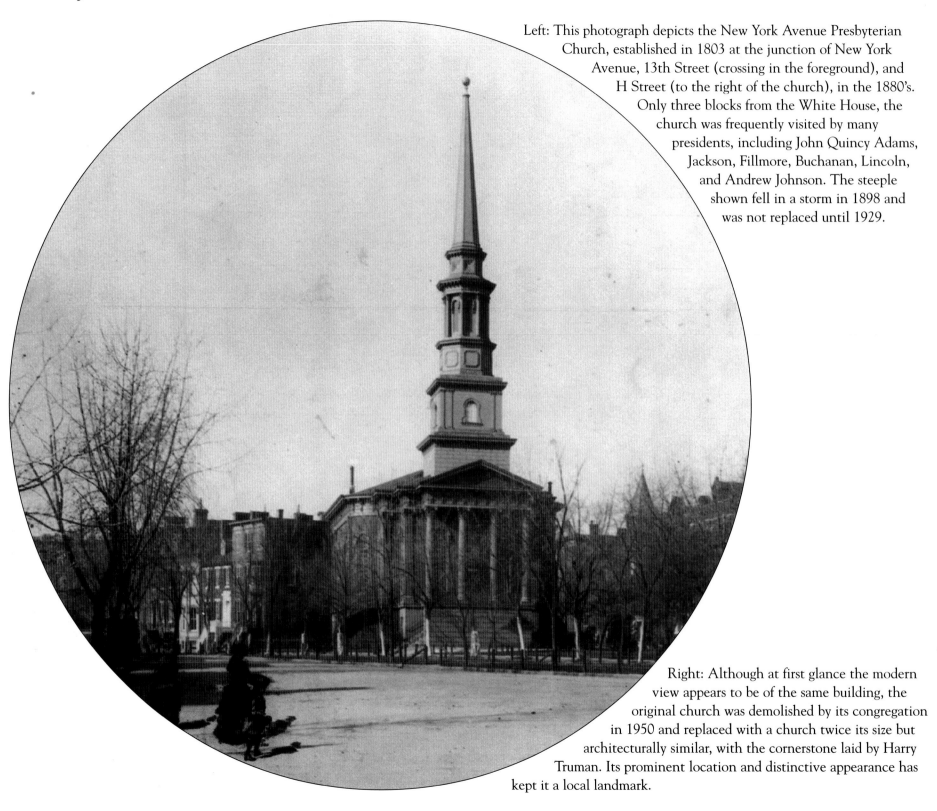

Left: This photograph depicts the New York Avenue Presbyterian Church, established in 1803 at the junction of New York Avenue, 13th Street (crossing in the foreground), and H Street (to the right of the church), in the 1880's. Only three blocks from the White House, the church was frequently visited by many presidents, including John Quincy Adams, Jackson, Fillmore, Buchanan, Lincoln, and Andrew Johnson. The steeple shown fell in a storm in 1898 and was not replaced until 1929.

Right: Although at first glance the modern view appears to be of the same building, the original church was demolished by its congregation in 1950 and replaced with a church twice its size but architecturally similar, with the cornerstone laid by Harry Truman. Its prominent location and distinctive appearance has kept it a local landmark.

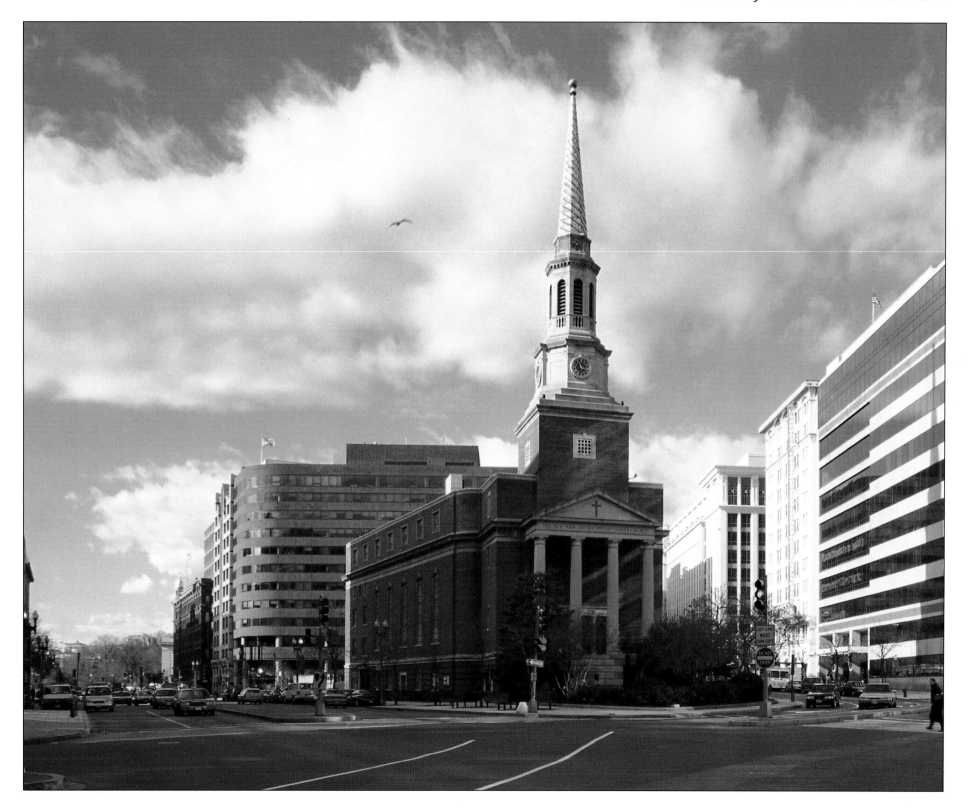

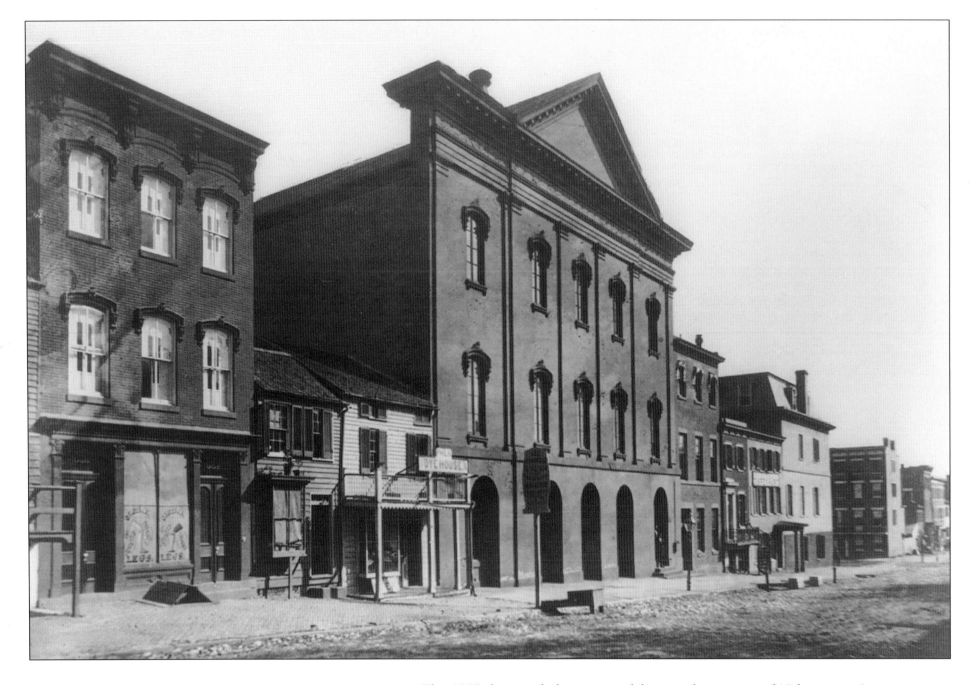

This 1865 photograph depicts one of the most famous sites of 19th century American history. Built in 1863 by John Ford in what was then a disreputable part of the city, it functioned as a theater for only two years when, on the night of April 14, 1865, John Wilkes Booth shot President Abraham Lincoln during the performance of *Our American Cousin*. It was destined to be the last theatrical performance at the theater until 1968. Lincoln was taken across the street to the Petersen House, where he died the next morning.

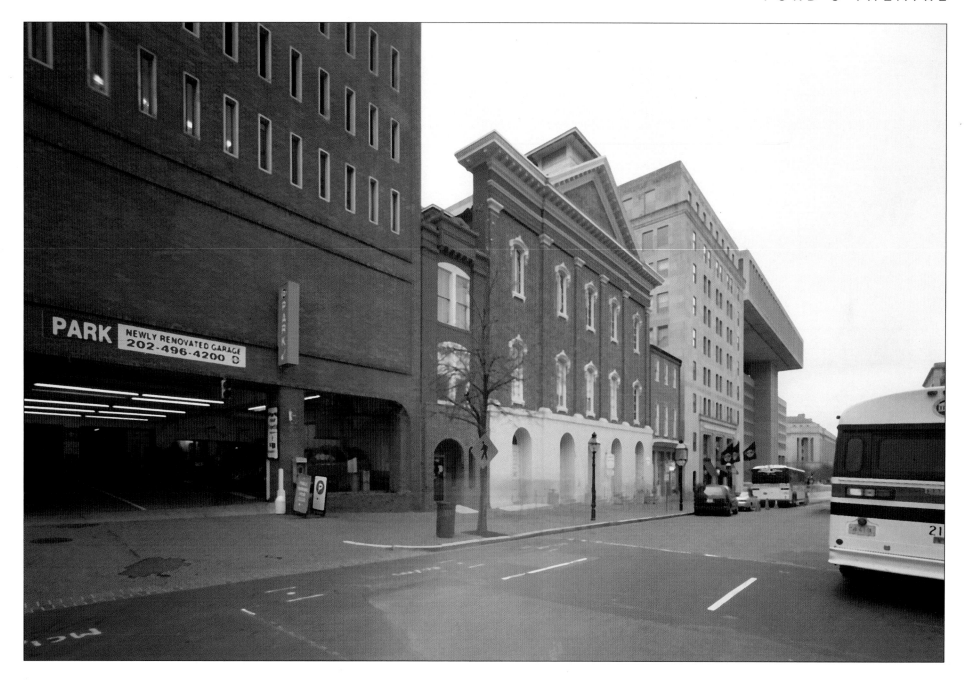

A year after the tragedy, the Federal government purchased the building and used it for
office and storage space; in 1893 tragedy struck again when part of the building collapsed,
killing 22 federal employees. The theater and the Petersen House are now operated by
the National Park Service with museums memorializing the death of Lincoln, and the
theater is used for occasional performances.

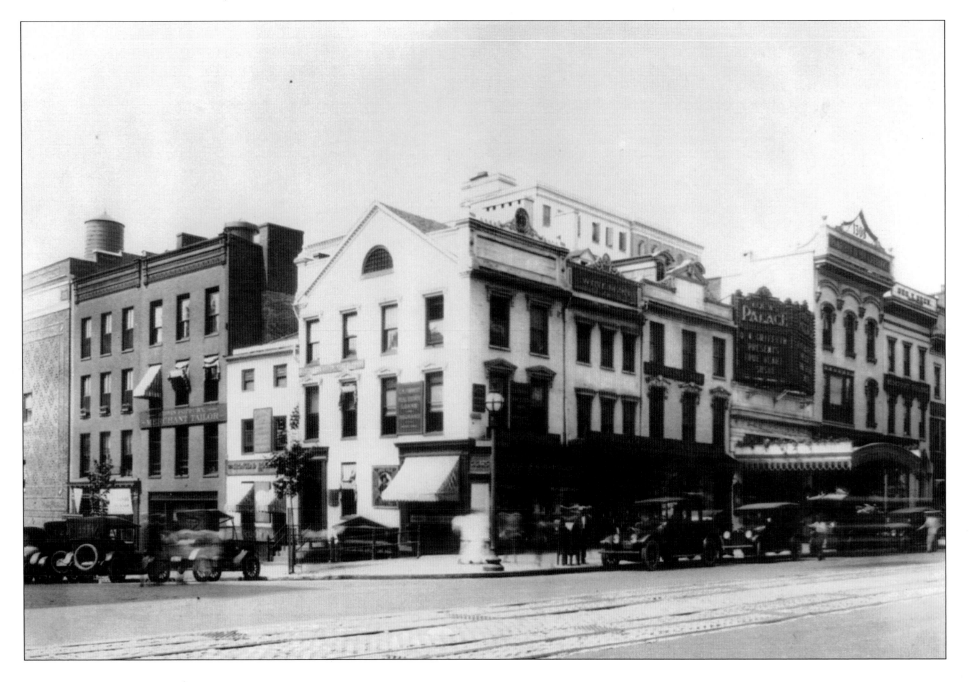

This humble corner is perhaps remarkable in downtown Washington as having nothing remarkable happen on the site. The Palace Theater, one of the city's early movie theaters, is visible, as are various commercial establishments. On the other side of the block behind these buildings is the National Theater, which had recently moved into a new building on Pennsylvania Avenue (which it still occupies).

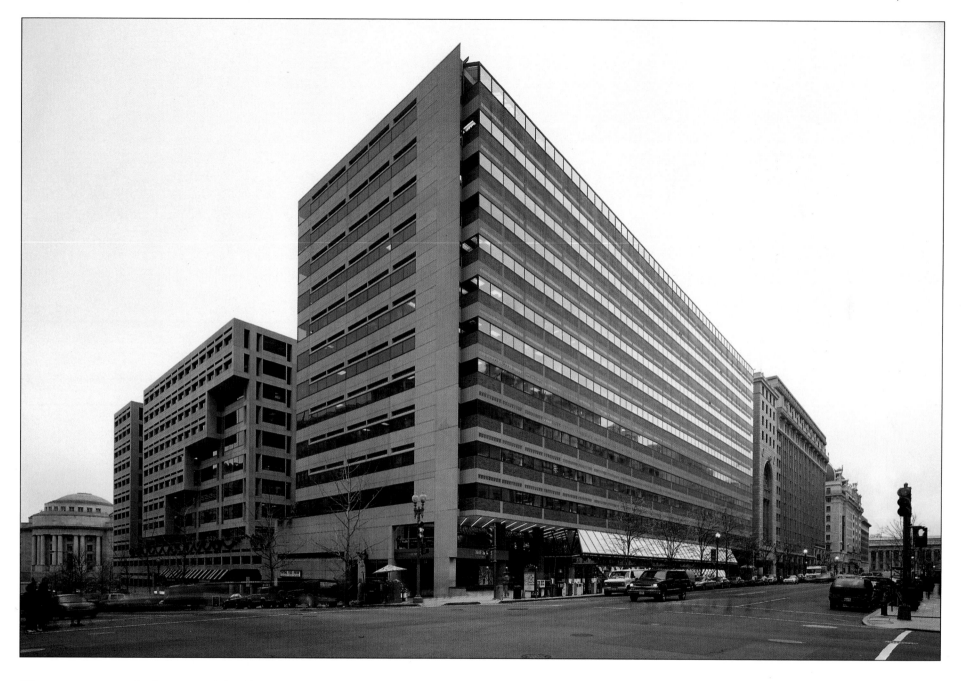

The corner is now the location of the Shops At National Place, an upscale shopping emporium just down the street from, and connected to, the National Press Building.

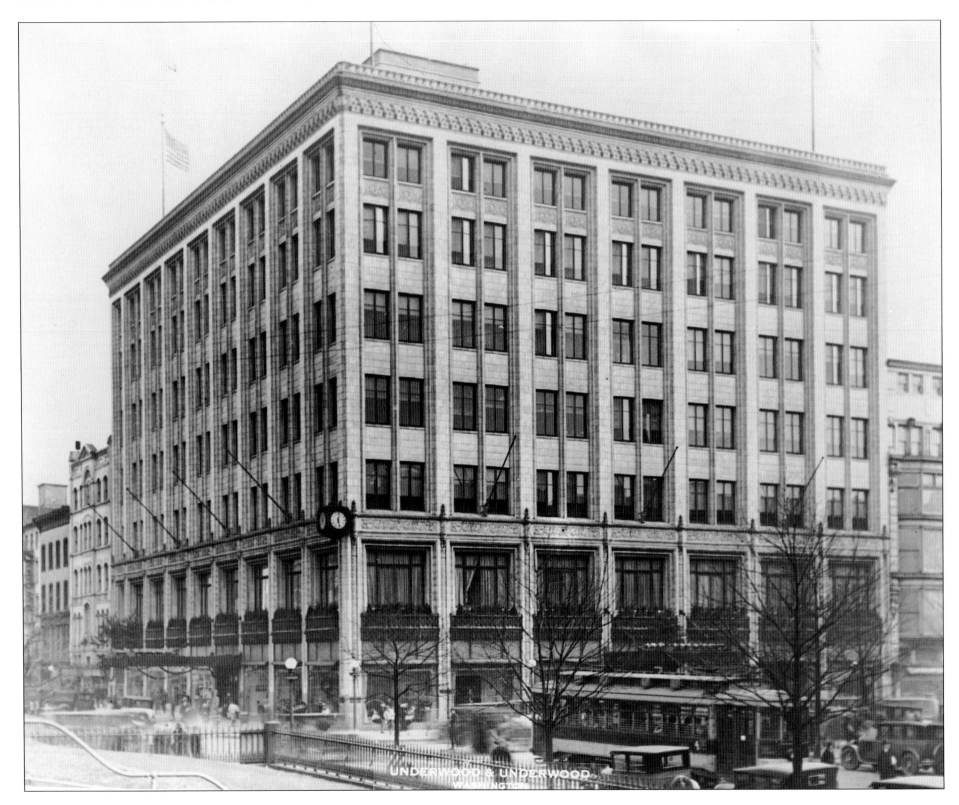

UNDERWOOD & UNDERWOOD
WASHINGTON

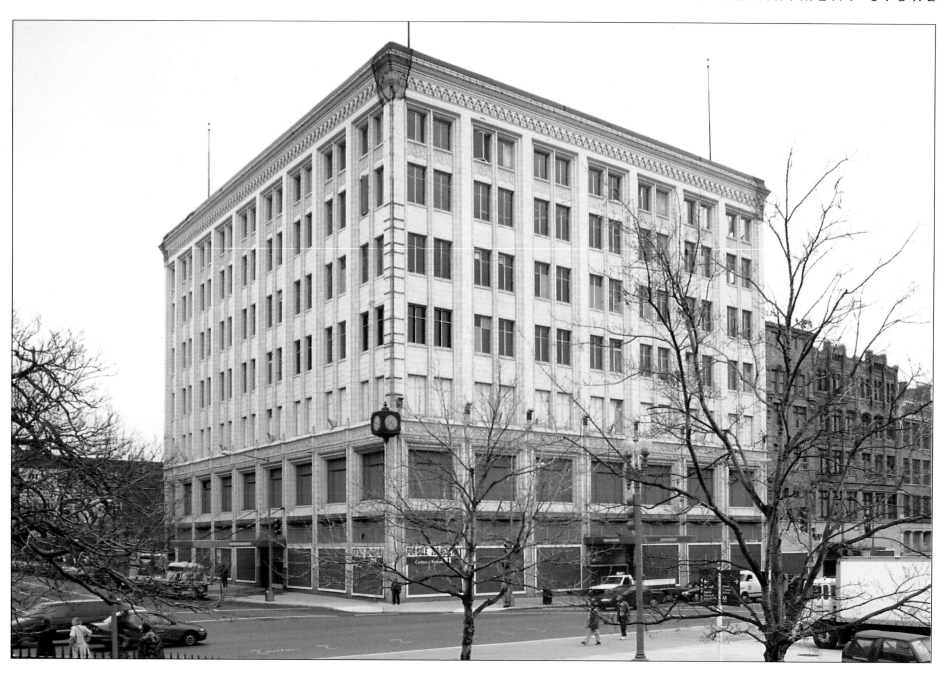

Left: Many department stores opened in the downtown commercial district around the turn of the 20th Century, including the Palais Royal on G Street between 10th and 11th streets, NW (which later evolved into the Woodward & Lothrop chain); Kann's ; Dulin & Martin at 1215 F Street (burned 1928) and this Hecht Company store, which was situated at the SE corner of 7th and F streets, NW.

Above: This location was picketed every Thursday night and Saturday beginning in June 1951 in protest of the store's denial of service to African-American customers at its lunch counter. The policy was lifted in January 1952. The Hecht Company, still a thriving local chain at this writing, moved from this location to nearby 8th & G streets in 1986; the building has been vacant since.

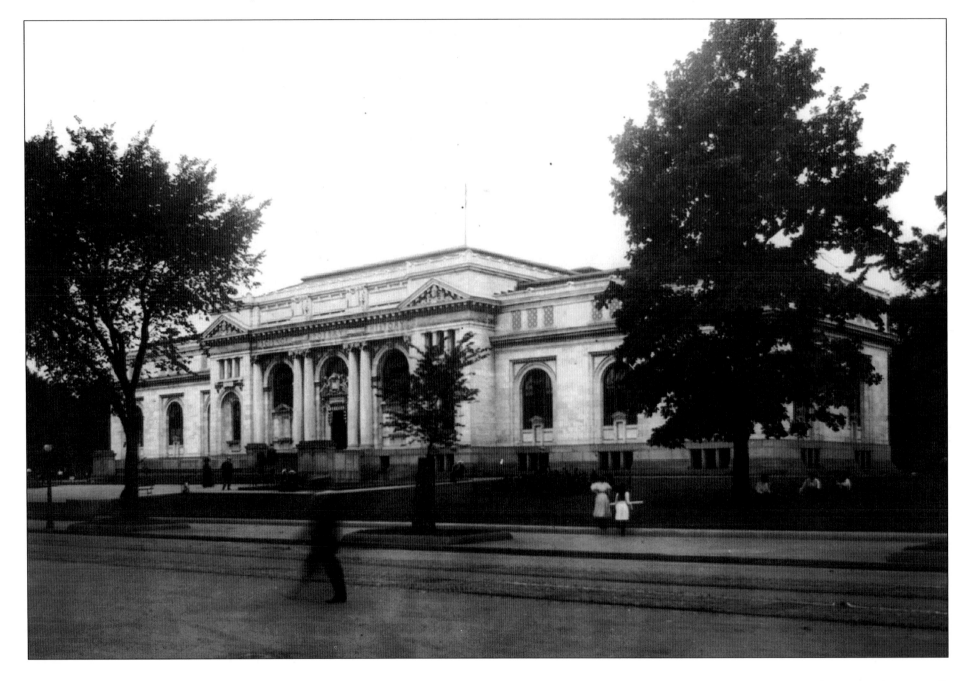

Located on Mt. Vernon Place at the junction of Massachusetts and New York avenues, this building was the contribution of noted American steelmaker-turned-philanthropist Andrew Carnegie. Occupying the site of the original Northern Liberty Market, it served as the original central public library of Washington from 1903 to 1972. This photograph dates back to 1910.

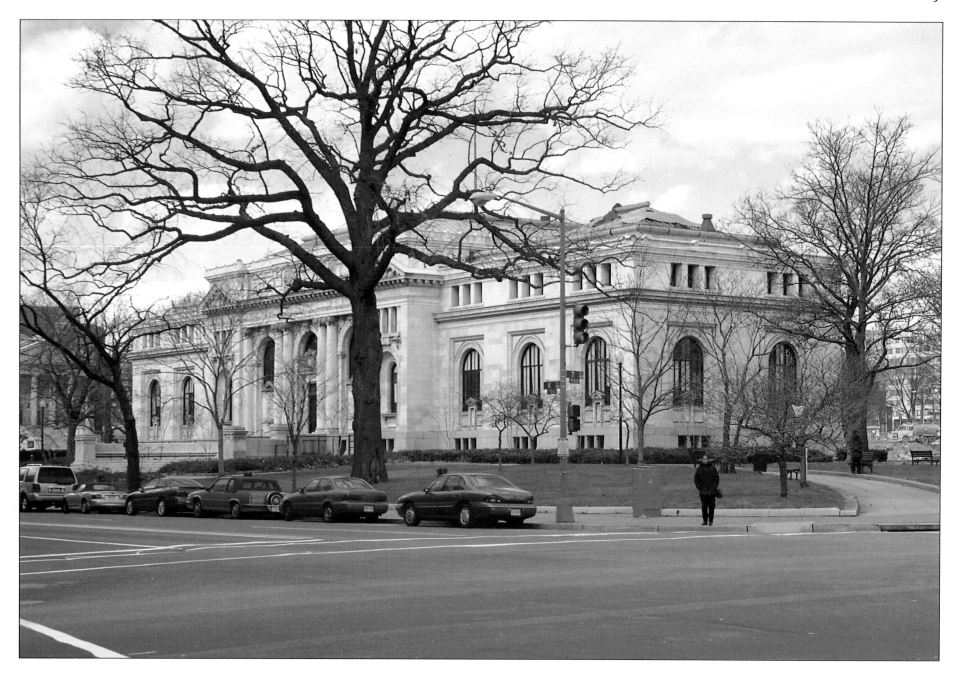

The building was used as the Carnegie Library by the University of the District of Columbia (founded in 1976 from a merger of three colleges) until 1998. It was then taken over as offices for construction of the new Washington Convention Center to the immediate north, to be completed in 2003. Plans are under way to establish the City Museum of Washington, D.C., a project of the Historical Society of Washington, D.C., in the building, to open at the same time as the convention center.

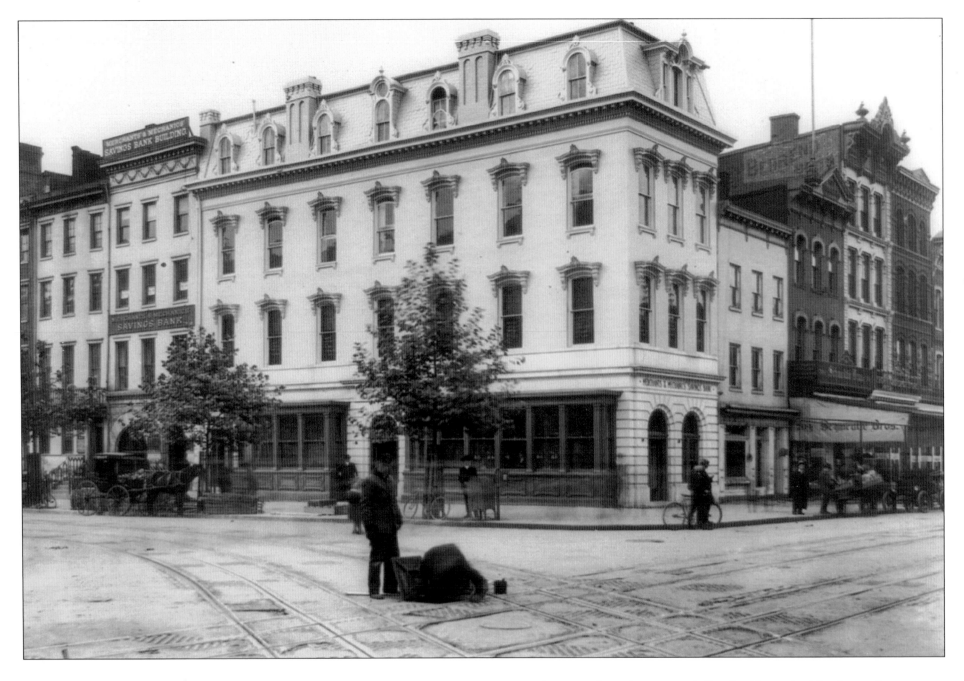

Across the street from the Patent Office Building, the Merchants & Mechanics Savings Bank, located in a building built in 1865, anchored another block of commercial establishments in the 7th Street shopping district. The men in the foreground are believed to be working on the below-street electrical conduits for streetcars. The photo was taken around 1910.

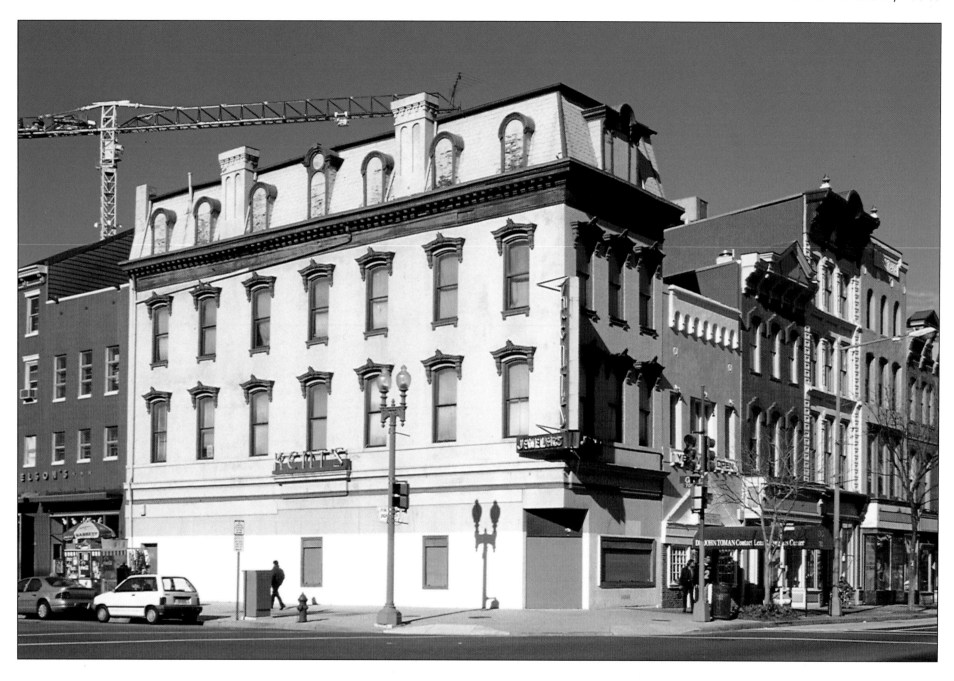

The corner building has held a variety of businesses, most recently a jewelry store that closed in the early 1990s as the MCI Center was opened across 7th Street. Almost the entire block of 7th Street was vacant at the time of the modern photo, when development was underway for the "7th Street Entertainment District" to occupy the block.

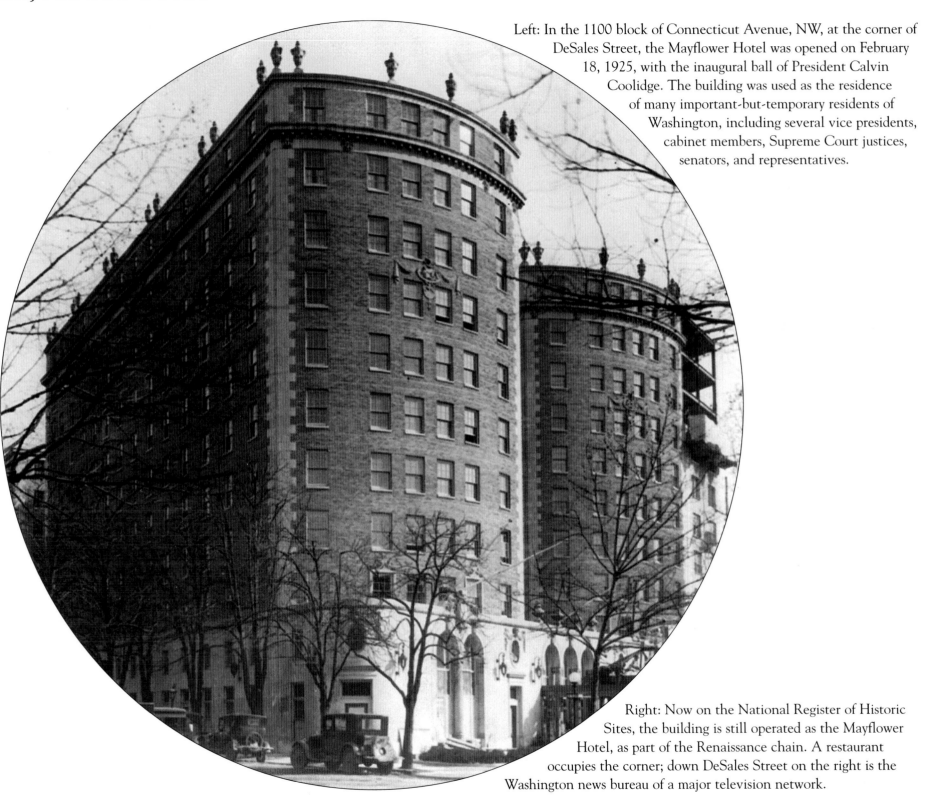

Left: In the 1100 block of Connecticut Avenue, NW, at the corner of DeSales Street, the Mayflower Hotel was opened on February 18, 1925, with the inaugural ball of President Calvin Coolidge. The building was used as the residence of many important-but-temporary residents of Washington, including several vice presidents, cabinet members, Supreme Court justices, senators, and representatives.

Right: Now on the National Register of Historic Sites, the building is still operated as the Mayflower Hotel, as part of the Renaissance chain. A restaurant occupies the corner; down DeSales Street on the right is the Washington news bureau of a major television network.

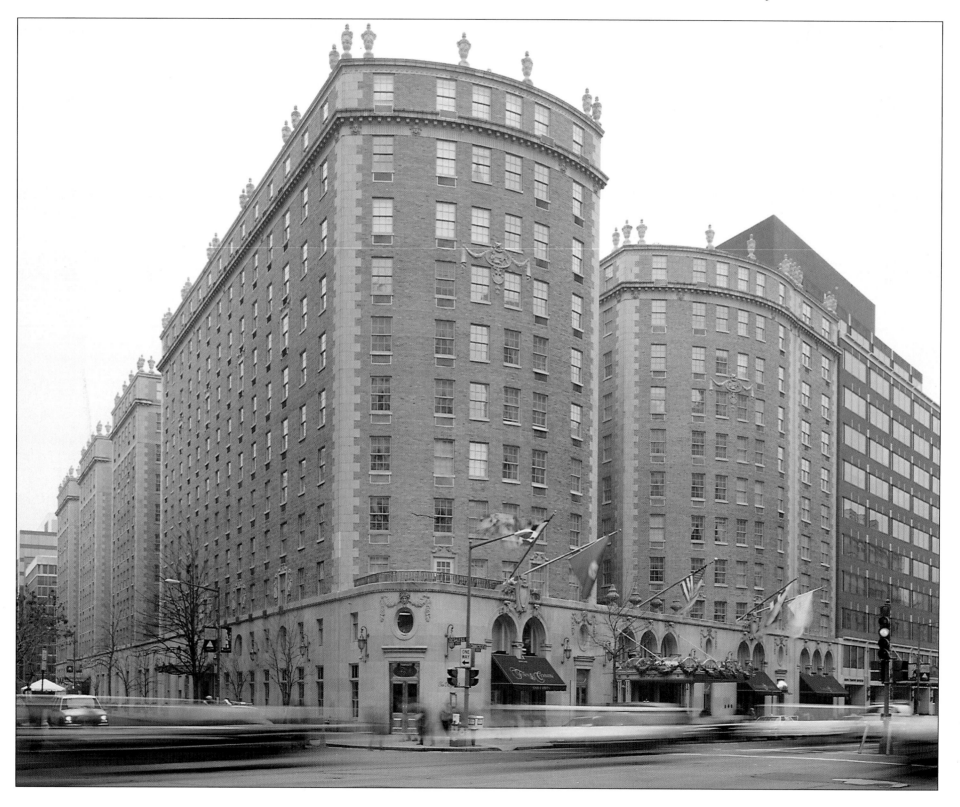

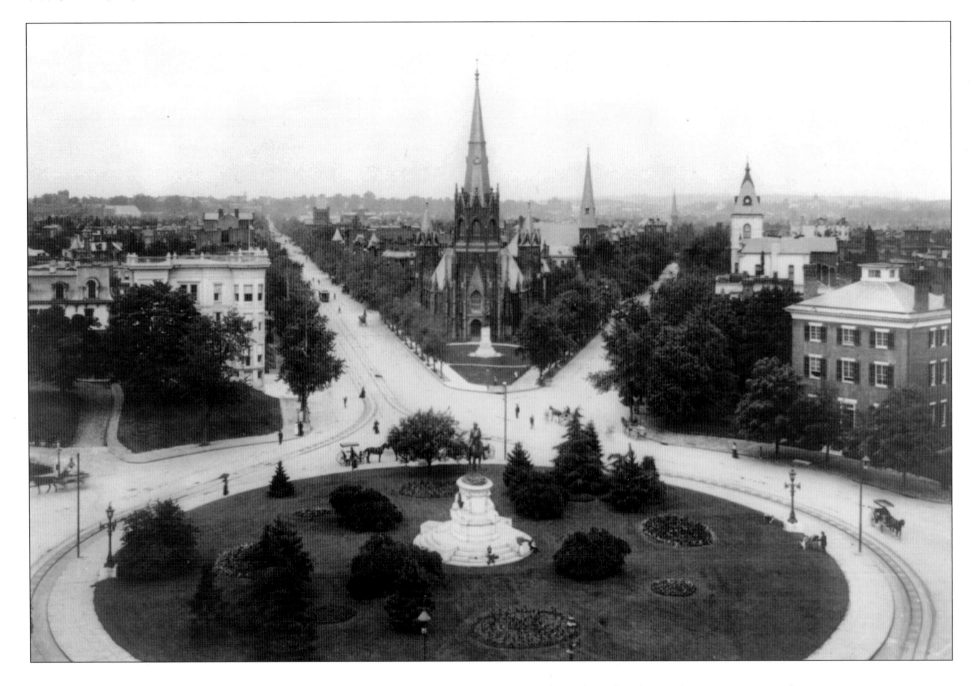

The original L'Enfant plan for Washington envisioned monuments or statues in each public square, to be erected by the states in memory of the military achievements or leaders that "were conspicuous in giving liberty and independence to this country." This photograph, from around 1890, was taken from the top of the Portland, the first apartment building in Washington, erected in 1879-80 and demolished in 1962; a modern hotel now occupies the site.

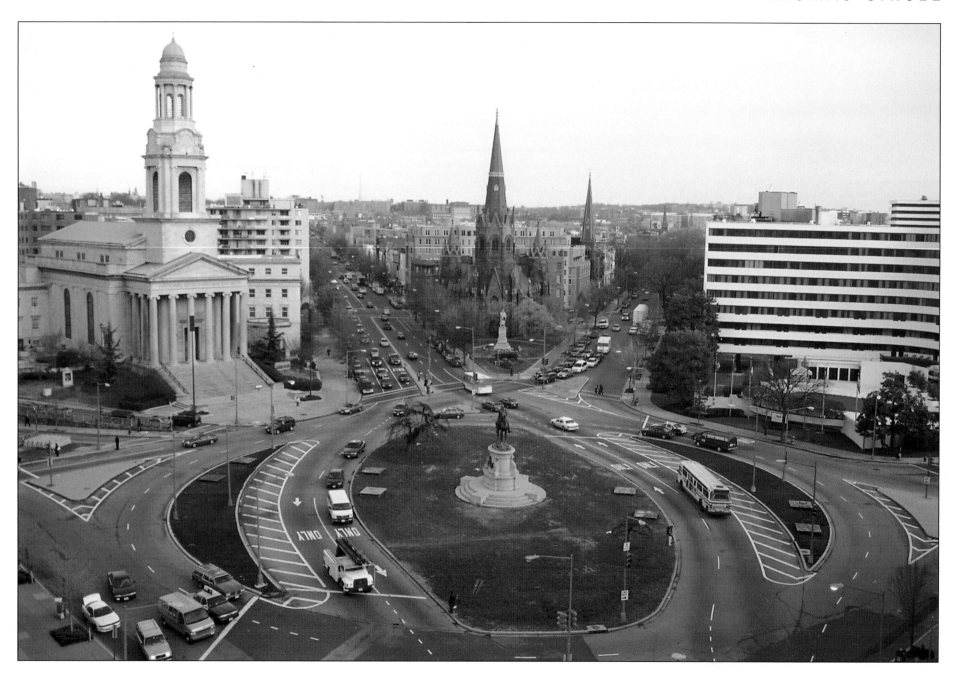

Today, the scene has changed considerably. But behind the statue can still be seen the Luther Place Memorial Church, built in 1870 as a thanksgiving to the end of the Civil War. To the left is the National City Christian Church, built in 1930 on the former home of Bishop Henry Y. Satterlee, the first Episcopal bishop of Washington (1896–1908), who planned and started the Washington National Cathedral.

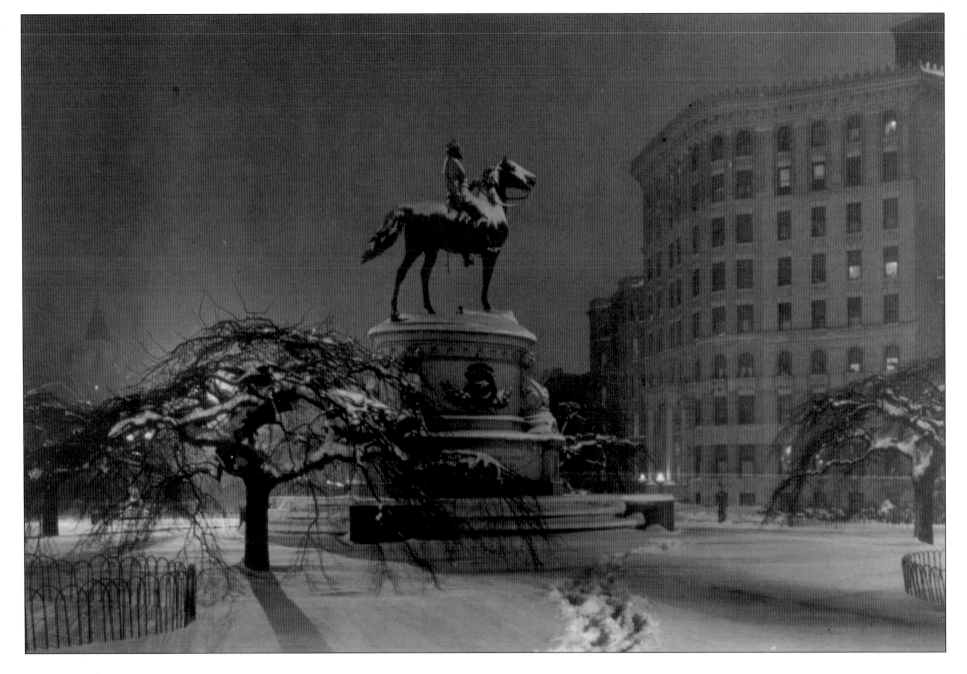

Major General George H. Thomas (1816–70) was a Union general in the Civil War, who earned the nickname "The Rock of Chickamauga" for his stand in the campaign for Chattanooga in September 1863. He later pursued the army of General John Hood through Tennessee, defeating them at the Battle of Nashville in December 1864. The circle at the junction of Massachusetts and Vermont avenues and M and 14th streets was named in his honor on November 19, 1879, with great pageantry and a parade lasting two hours.

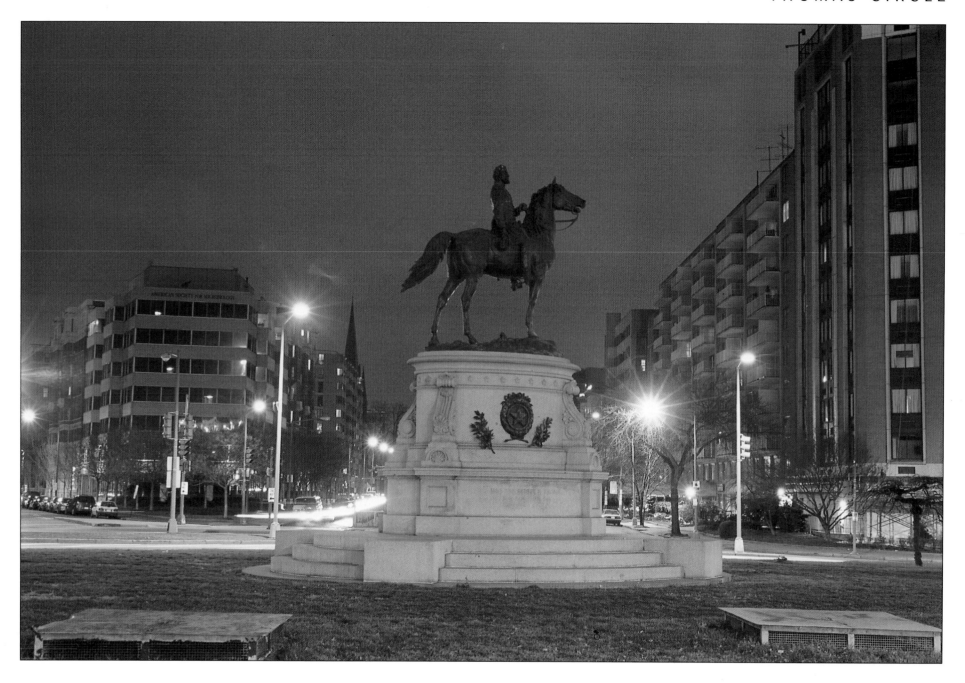

Massachusetts Avenue, which formerly passed through the circle at street level, now passes through a tunnel directly underneath the circle—a traffic-expediting strategy now common at many of the city's circles. Although the quiet peace of the vintage photograph has been shattered by bright streetlights and traffic, the statue of General George H. Thomas still stands in the center of the circle named for him.

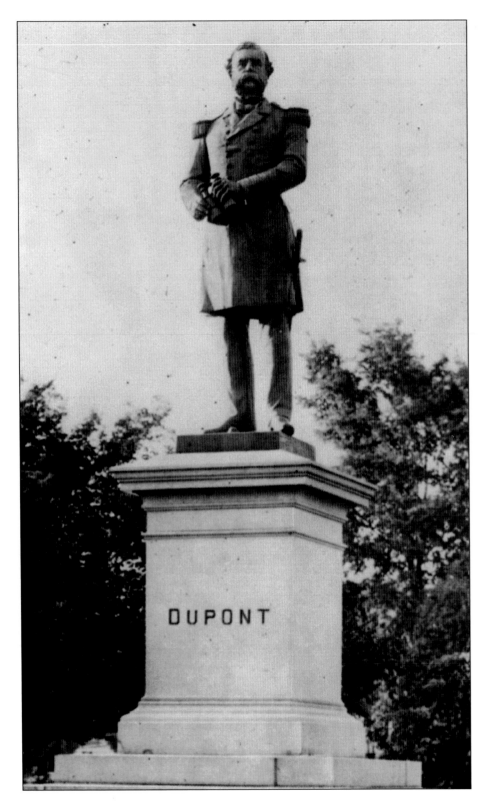

DUPONT

In a city not well-known for spontaneity or nightlife, the Dupont Circle neighborhood at 19th and P streets, NW, is perhaps the thriving hub of Washingtonian entertainment and spectacle, the closest the city has to Times Square or Piccadilly. The only trace of its namesake, however is an inscription on the edge of this present-day fountain. This statue of Civil War hero Admiral Samuel Francis Dupont (1803–65) was erected in 1884 at the circle of Massachusetts Avenue, M Street, and New Hampshire Avenue, which was formerly known as Pacific Circle.

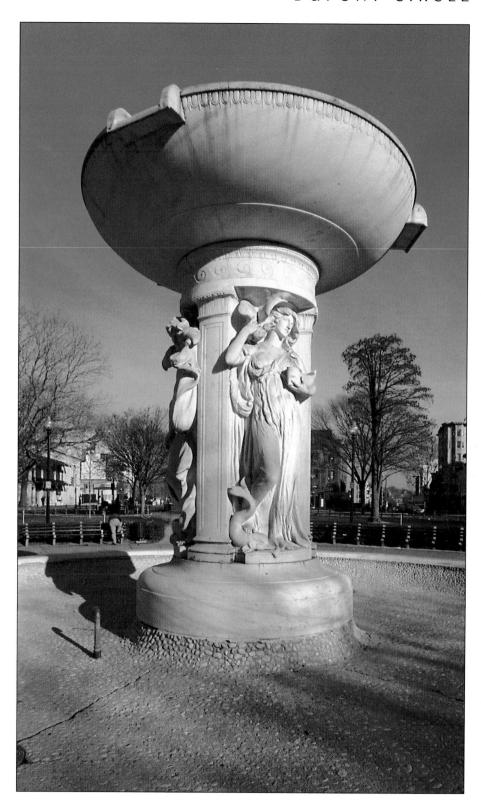

The Dupont family, who had founded what became the Dupont corporation, became upset with the statue's neglect and removed the statue to the family hometown of Wilmington, Delaware. They then commissioned Daniel Chester French to design the marble fountain, dedicated in 1921, which occupies the circle today, with its allegorical figures of Sea, Stars, and Wind.

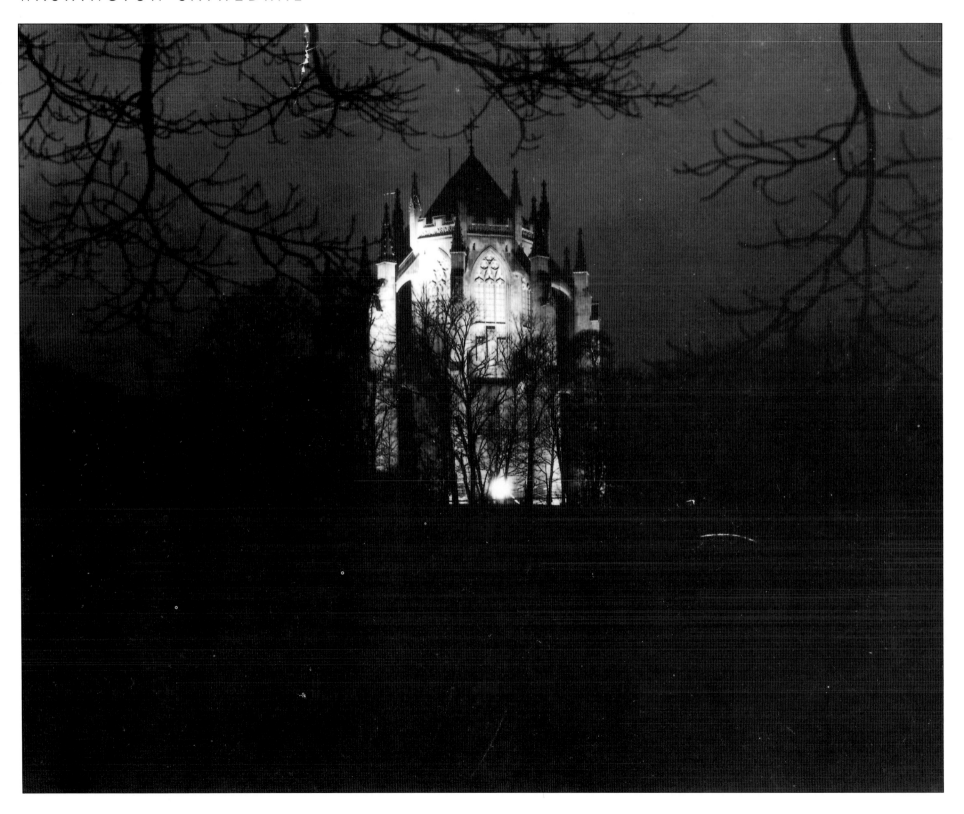

Left: The Cathedral Church of St. Peter and Paul, also known as the Washington National Cathedral, was built on the site of Mt. Alban, a plot of land purchased in 1813 by Joseph Nourse, an English native who named the property after his birthplace of Mount Saint Alban in Hertfordshire. A deeply religious man, he wanted his property used for a church, and St. Albans Episcopal Church opened in 1852. By the 1900s plans had advanced for a Gothic cathedral on the property, among the highest points in the District, and construction began in 1907 with the laying of a foundation stone by Theodore Roosevelt.

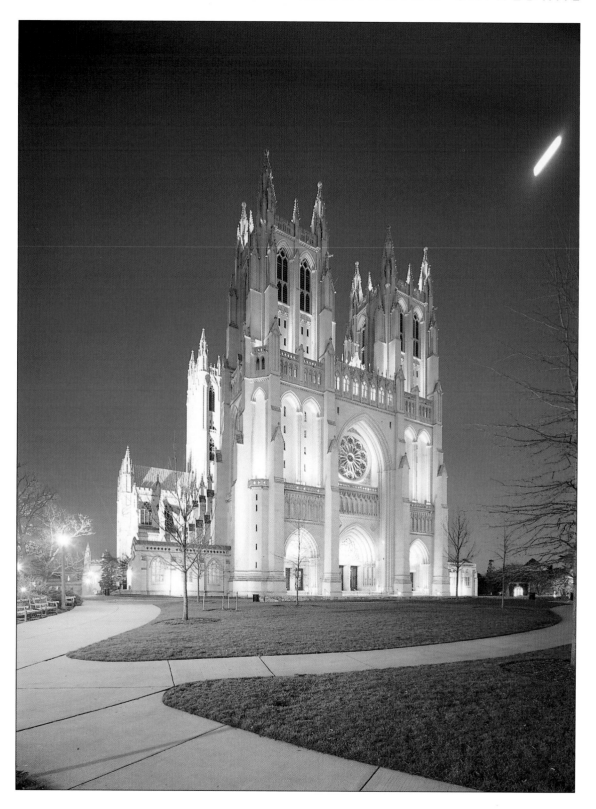

Right: By 1990 the Cathedral had been essentially completed, and a dedication and consecration ceremony was held in September of that year. It now houses the tomb of Woodrow Wilson, the only President buried in Washington.

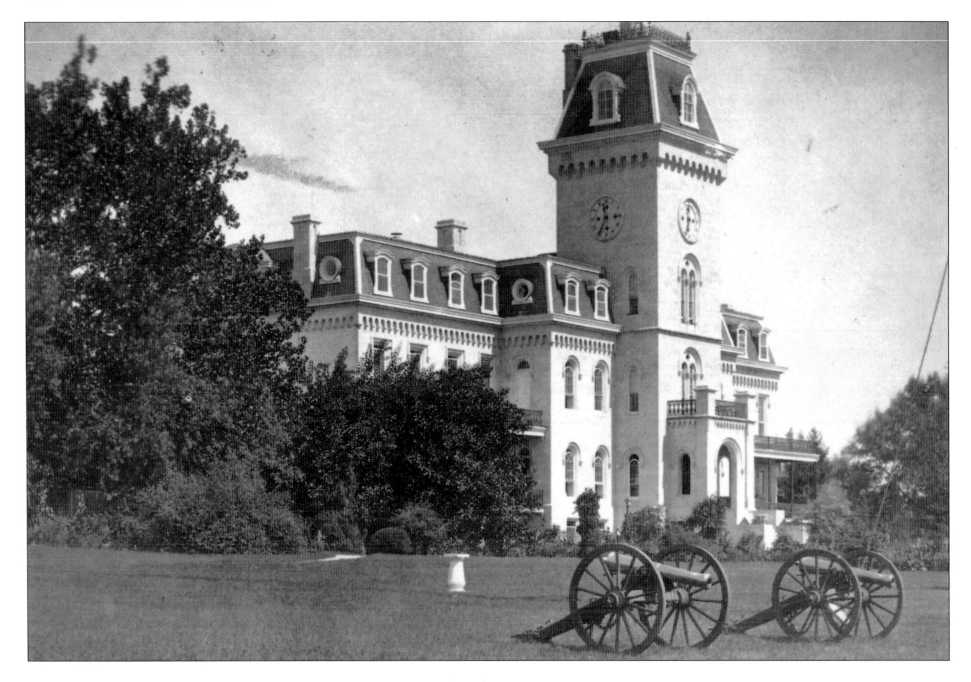

Established in 1851 by General Winfield Scott as the Soldiers' Home, this hospital and its sprawling grounds sit in the far northern section of the District. To the left is the Anderson Cottage, also known as Corn Riggs or the Presidents' Cottage, built by banker George Washington Riggs in 1843 and destined to be the first building of the home. It was also used as a summer home by several presidents, including Buchanan and Lincoln, in an attempt to escape the District's stifling summer humidity and heat in the days before air conditioning.

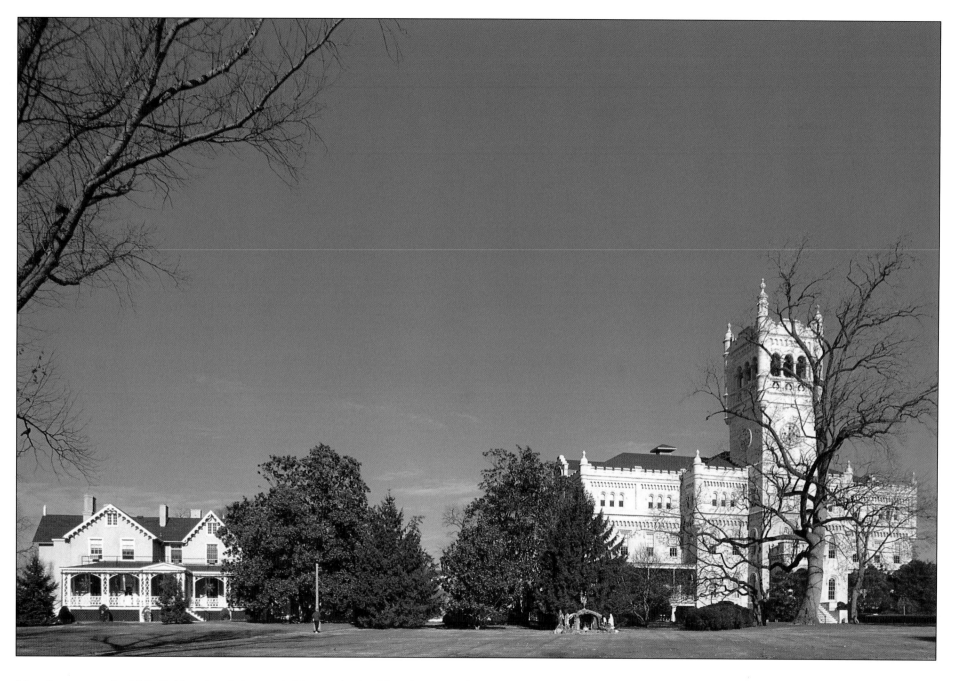

Now known as the U.S. Soldiers' and Airmen's Home, the building has served for over a 100 years in the role for which it was founded, as a nursing home and hospital for military personnel who have either been injured or have served for at least 20 years. Many more modern buildings also occupy the grounds as well.

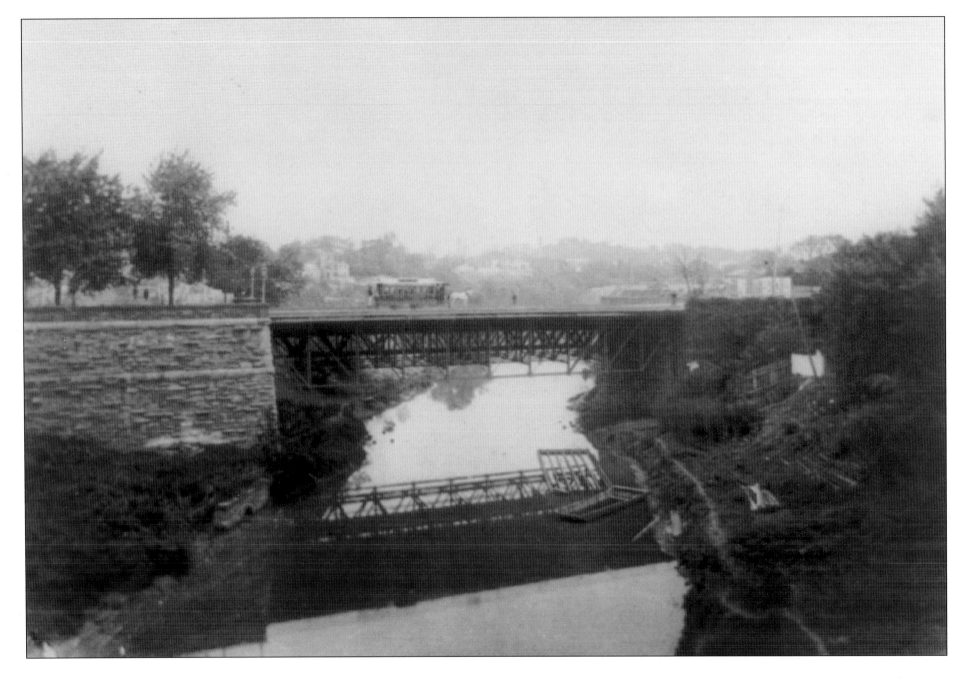

Originally a prosperous separate entity that arose from an early 1700s tobacco-trading port on the Potomac, Georgetown formally became part of the District of Columbia in 1878. This iron bridge carried M Street (and horsecar and streetcar lines—note the horsecar) across Rock Creek just north of the junction of the creek and the Chesapeake & Ohio Canal. At the time Rock Creek was still navigable at its lower end, and it was earlier used as a canal-boat staging area. It is seen from the Pennsylvania Avenue bridge, built atop water-supply conduits still in place today.

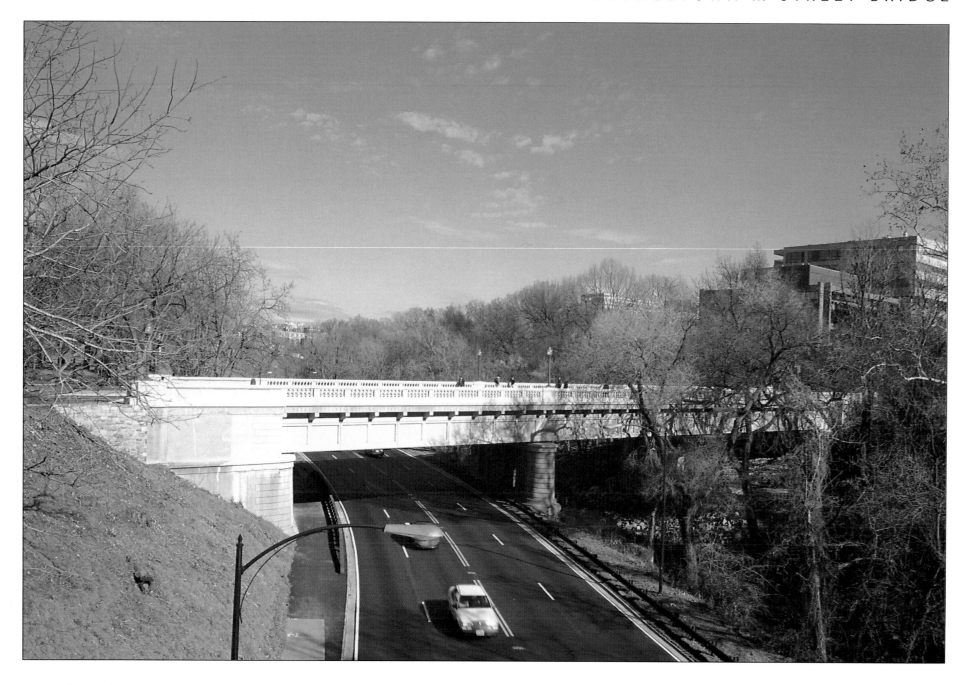

Today the southern end of the Rock Creek & Potomac Parkway, a major commuter artery from the north, which ends behind our vantage point, shares the underside of the successor bridge with a considerably less navigable Rock Creek, which is just visible behind the trees on the right of the photograph.

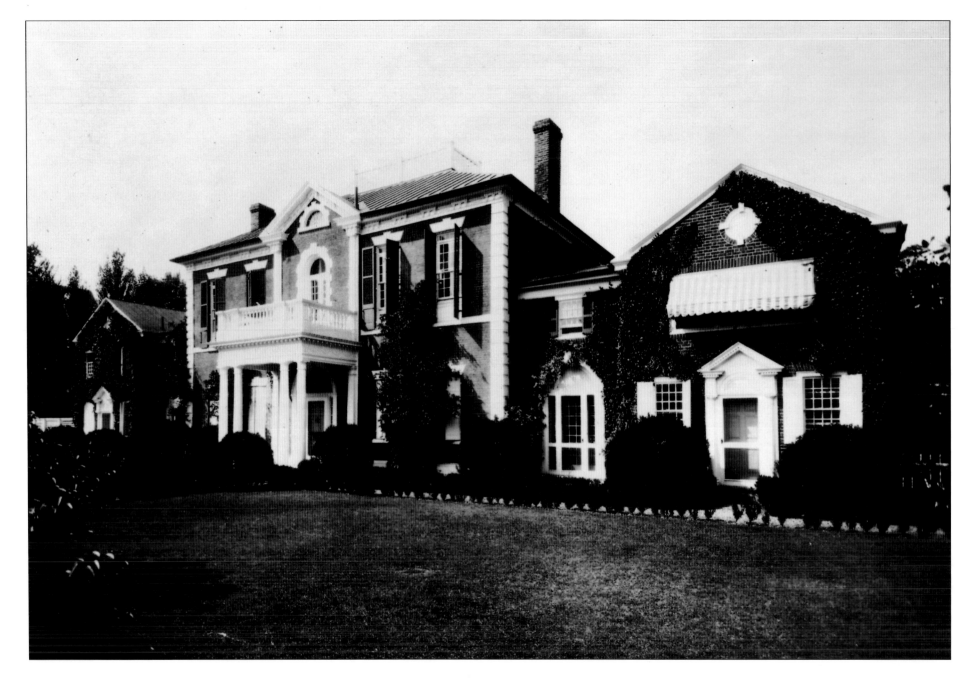

Built in 1799 by Samuel Jackson and originally called Bellevue, this house was one of the first of what would be many grand houses to rise on the heights of Georgetown overlooking the Potomac. The property changed hands many times before and after the house was built, in the rapid real estate speculation surrounding the founding of the federal city. During the War of 1812 it was owned by Charles Carroll of Bellevue, who evacuated Dolley Madison to this house when the British burned the White House in 1814.

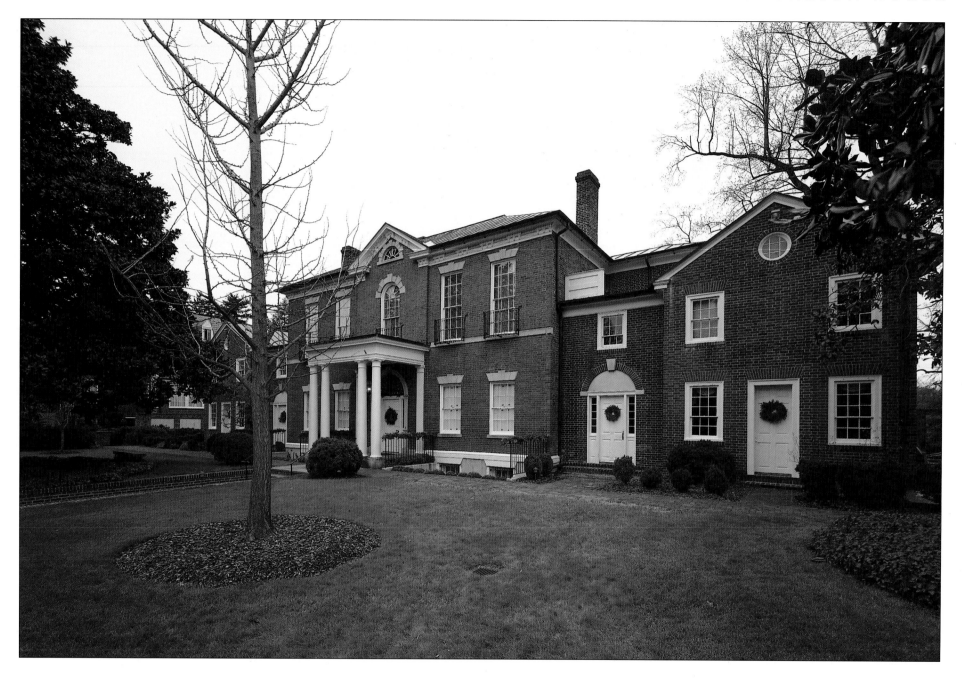

Moved slightly from its original spot in 1915 to allow for the extension of Q Street, the Dumbarton House at 2715 Q Street is now preserved as a museum and headquarters of the National Society of the Colonial Dames of America.

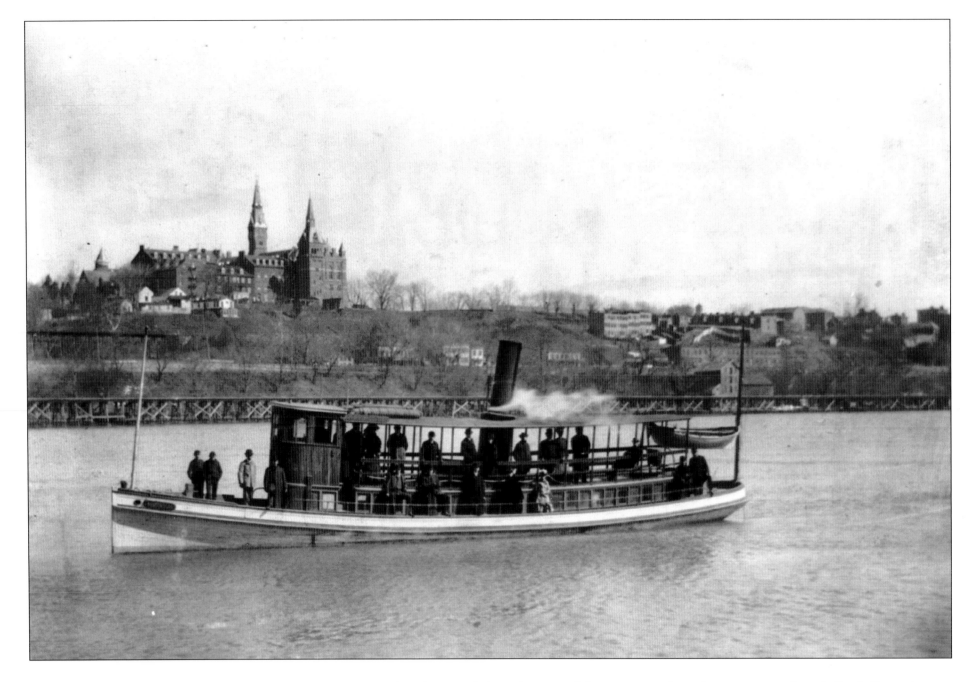

Seen in this photograph from the turn of the century is the sightseeing steam launch *Bartholdi* on the Potomac River west of the Aqueduct Bridge, with Georgetown on the opposite shore. Founded in 1789, Georgetown University was the first Catholic university in the United States. The tall spires mark newly completed Healy Hall (1879). To the right on the far shore can be seen the Washington Canoe Club, built around 1890. The trestling on the far side of the river is probably the Washington & Great Falls Electric Railway extending to Glen Echo Park via this alignment parallel to the C&O Canal.

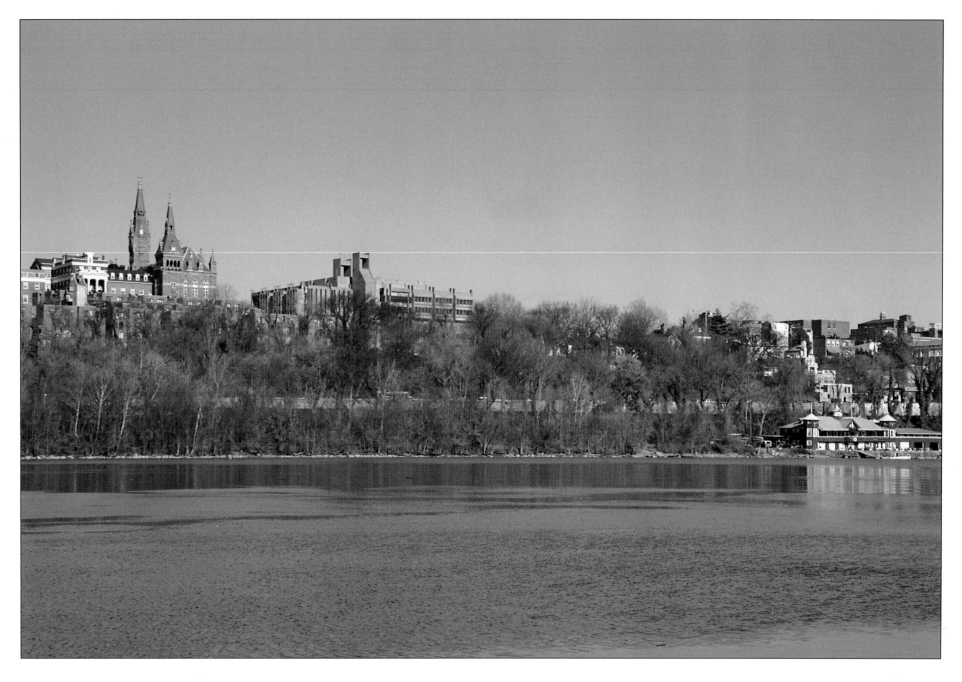

Today a four-lane highway, an important connector between Georgetown and the northwestern suburbs, hides behind the trees on the opposite shore. Healy Hall and other newer buildings of Georgetown University still offer a spectacular view of the Potomac River.

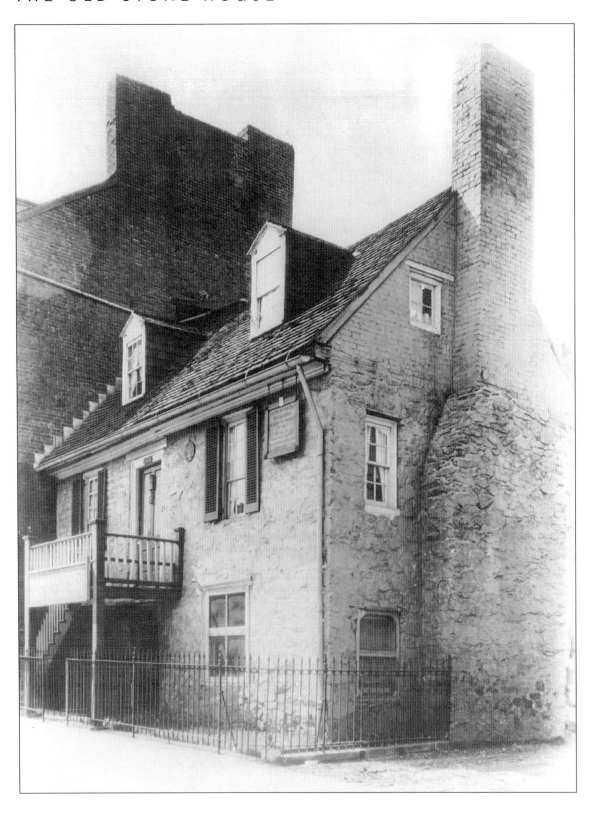

Built about 1765 by cabinetmaker Christopher Layman, this old stone six-room house at Jefferson and M streets is regarded as the oldest (and only precolonial) building in the District. Local legend had the building as the site of the Washington meeting with L'Enfant to plan the city, but this has since been refuted. It originally served as a carpentry shop and home for Layman and his family.

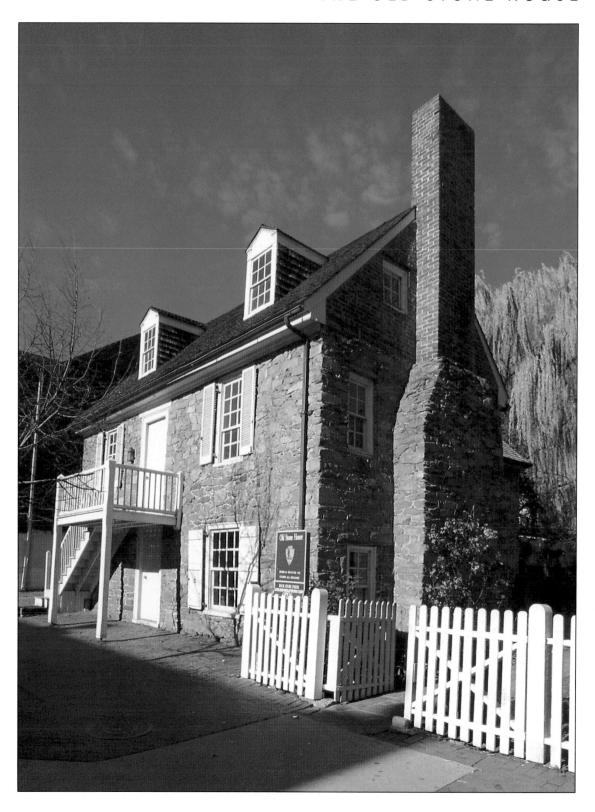

In later years the house served as a commercial establishment, ending up as a sign-painting shop and finally a used-car dealer's lot and office. It is now maintained by the National Park Service as a museum to the modest lifestyle and living of everyday colonial Americans, complete with period furnishings.

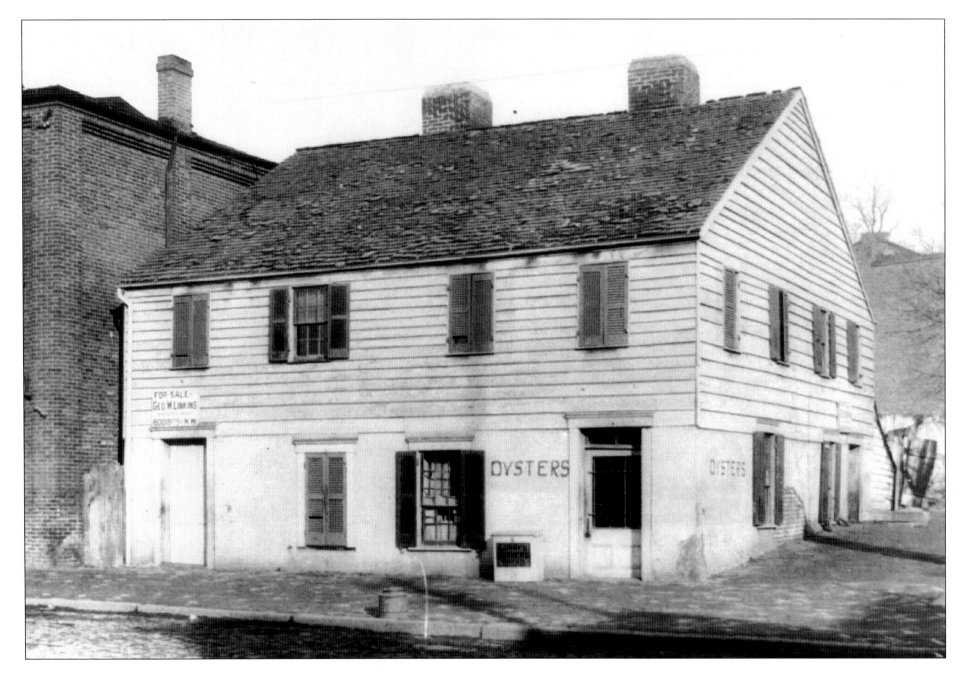

On March 30, 1791, the owners of the properties that would become the District of Columbia met with George Washington at Suter's Tavern in Georgetown. They agreed to sell their land to the government for $66.67 an acre and the ownership of half the building lots in the new city. Unfortunately, the exact location of this tavern has been lost to the ages. This particular colonial-era tavern at 31st and K streets, said to be a leading contender because it vaguely matched later drawings of the building, was demolished in 1931 to make way for a city incinerator.

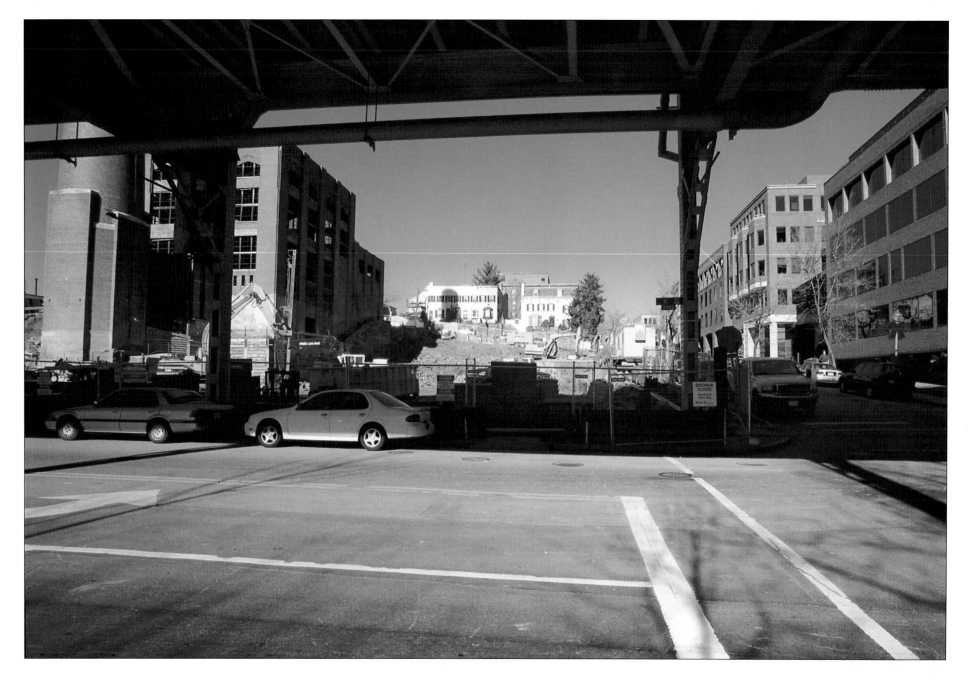

The site now sits in the shadow of the elevated Whitehurst Freeway, built in 1949. The incinerator itself closed in 1971, and as the 20th century came to a close, the location was part of the last undeveloped plot of land in Georgetown, being developed as a $150 million luxury hotel, shopping, and 12-screen theater complex. Ironically, the incinerator with its 163-foot smokestack, a source of fumes and derision over decades, is now itself the subject of preservation efforts due to its Art Deco architecture.

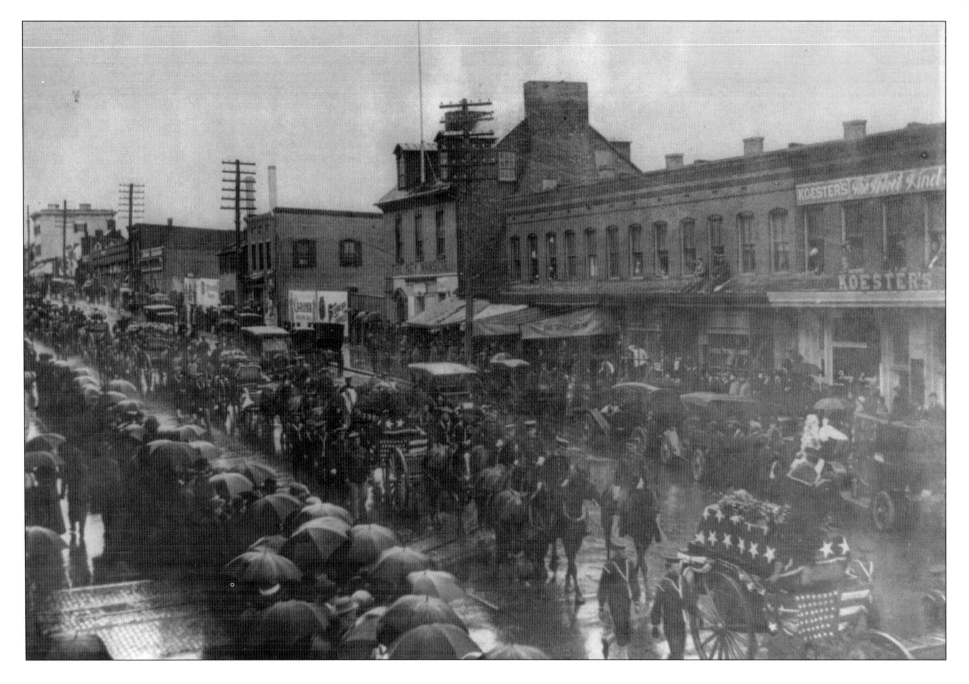

In 1912, the unidentified bodies of 64 sailors were recovered from the wreckage of the U.S.S. *Maine*, which had exploded in Havana harbor in 1896 and thus launched the United States into the Spanish-American War. Here, the funeral procession for these sailors moves down M Street in Georgetown *en route* to the Aqueduct Bridge and Arlington National Cemetery. In the center of the photograph can be seen the Key Mansion, the onetime residence of Francis Scott Key, an attorney and the author of "The Star-Spangled Banner."

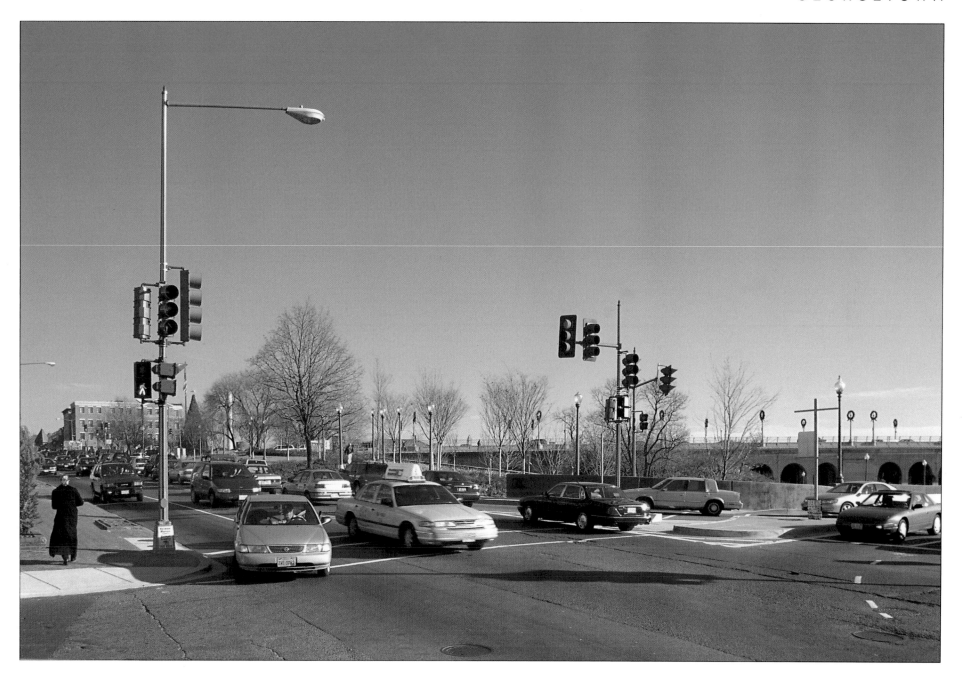

Built in 1802 and later operated as a museum, the Key Mansion was unfortunately demolished in 1948–49 (despite promises to dismantle and rebuild the structure) to make way for a ramp for the Whitehurst Freeway. The ramp itself is now itself history, but the adjacent Francis Scott Key Bridge, built to replace the Aqueduct Bridge that originally carried the C&O Canal, retains the name.

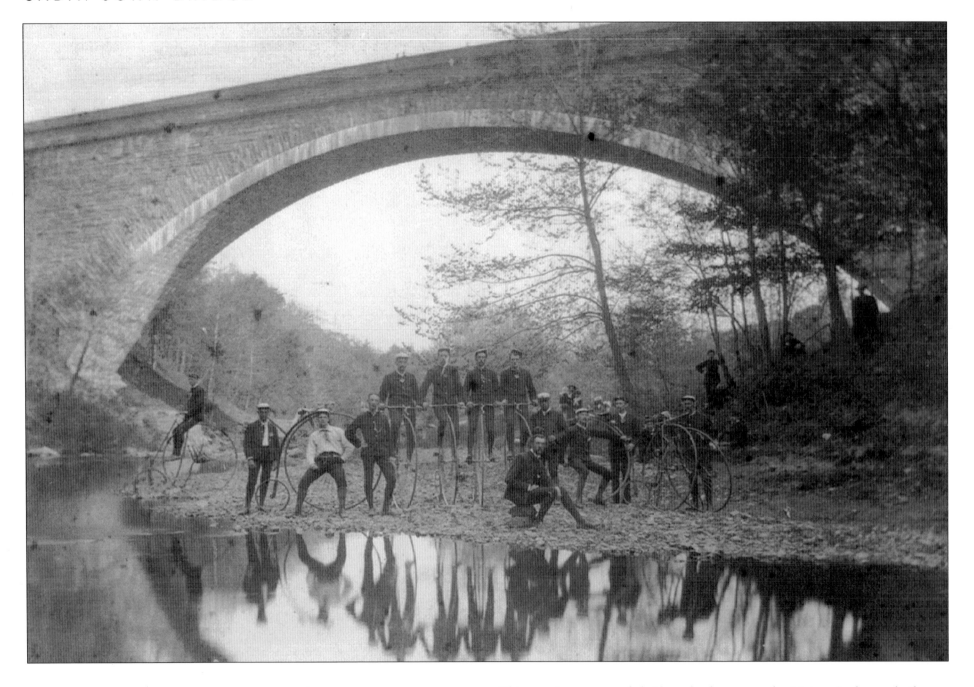

This massive stone-arch bridge, also known as the Union Arch, was built between 1853 and 1864 by Montgomery C. Meigs as part of the water-supply aqueduct supplying Washington with water from the Cabin John Reservoir. With a clear span of 218 feet, it was the longest stone-arch span in the world for 40 years. The photograph dates from about 1890.

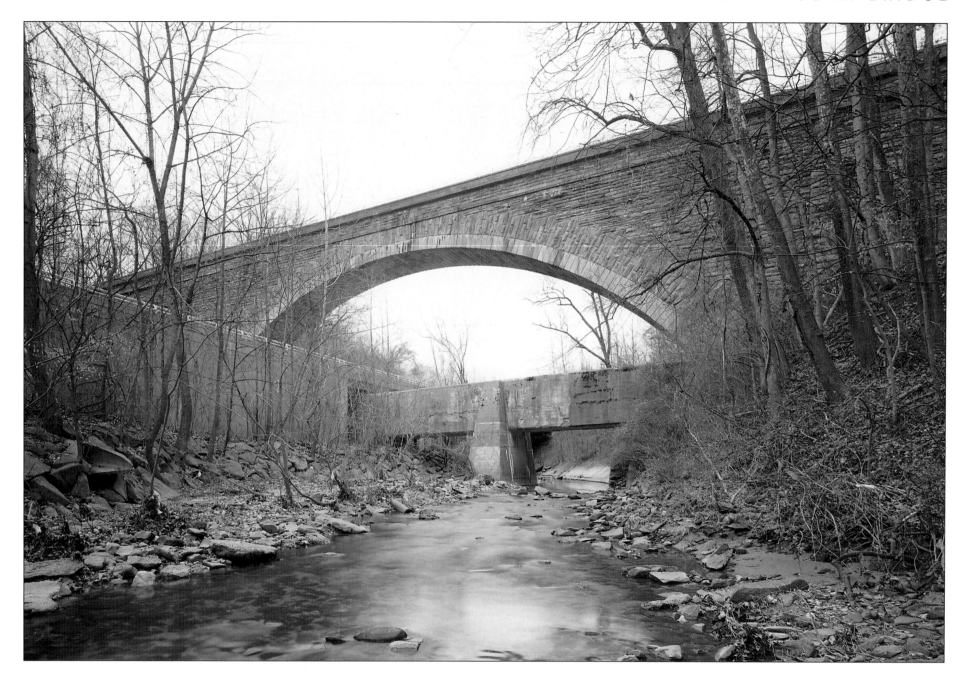

Today the bridge carries one lane at a time of MacArthur Boulevard over both Cabin John Creek and the parallel Cabin John Parkway (atop the tall wall to the left) connecting with the nearby Capital Beltway (I-495). The formerly pastoral location of the earlier photo is now all but inaccessible beneath the Parkway and the additional water aqueduct in the foreground.

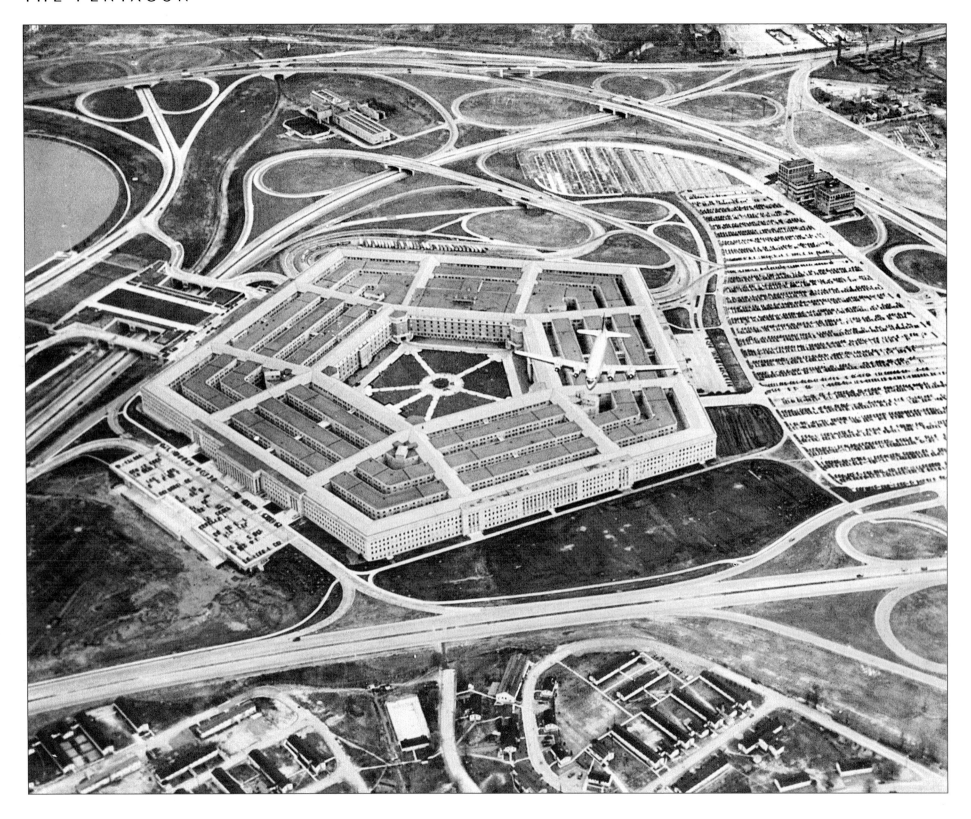

Left: The municipality now known as Arlington County was ceded to the federal government by Virginia in 1790, and was part of the District of Columbia until returned to Virginia in 1847; it was named in 1920. In this 1945 view of the Pentagon building the roads, approaches, and "clover-leaf" intersections make an intricate pattern.

Right: Completed in 1943 after only two years of construction, the Pentagon, the headquarters for the U.S. Department of Defense, remains the largest office building in the world, with 23,000 military and civilian employees occupying five concentric interconnected buildings with 17 miles of corridors covering a total of 34 acres.

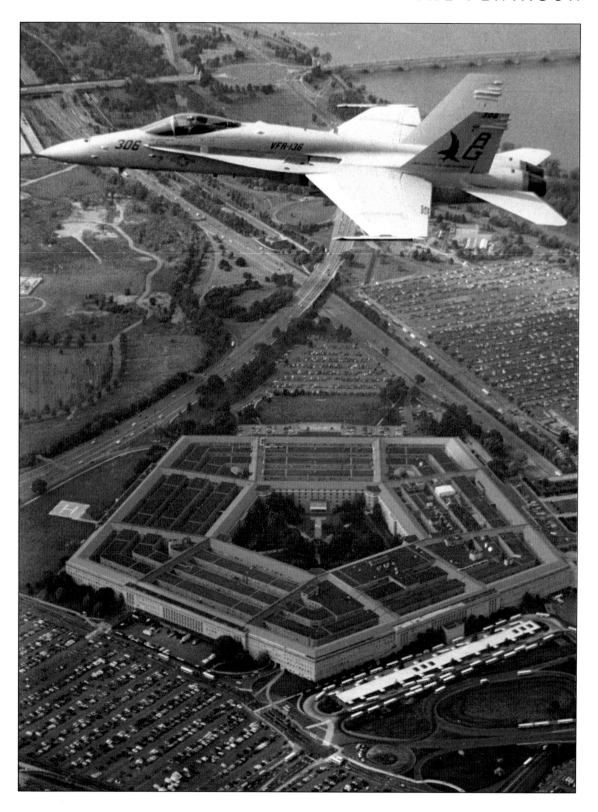

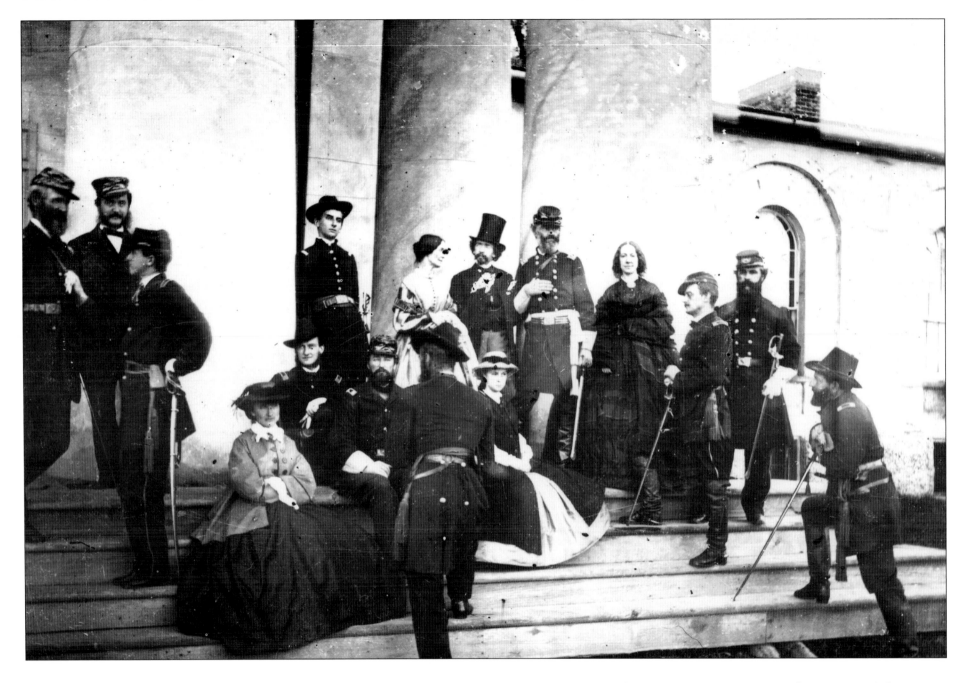

The Arlington National Cemetery was begun in 1864 on 200 acres of property in Arlington, Virginia, belonging to the family of Robert E. Lee (inherited by his wife), which included the mansion known as Arlington House. Lee and family abandoned the property early in the Civil War, and it was seized for nonpayment of taxes and even used as headquarters for the Union Army. The photograph shows Union soldiers on the steps of the house. Custis Lee, an heir, sued the government after the war, and was awarded $150,000 for title to the land.

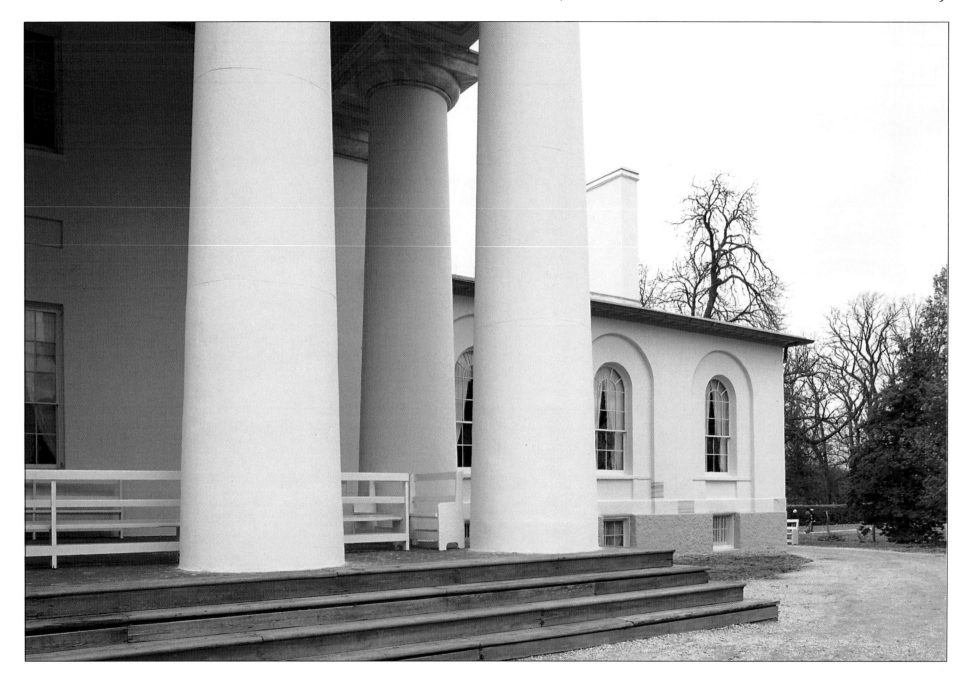

Arlington is today the largest and best-known of over one hundred national cemeteries, the final resting place for over 245,000 servicemen and their relatives. Today Arlington House is preserved and restored as the Robert E. Lee Memorial, which overlooks the graves of Civil War unknown soldiers and the grave of John F. Kennedy.

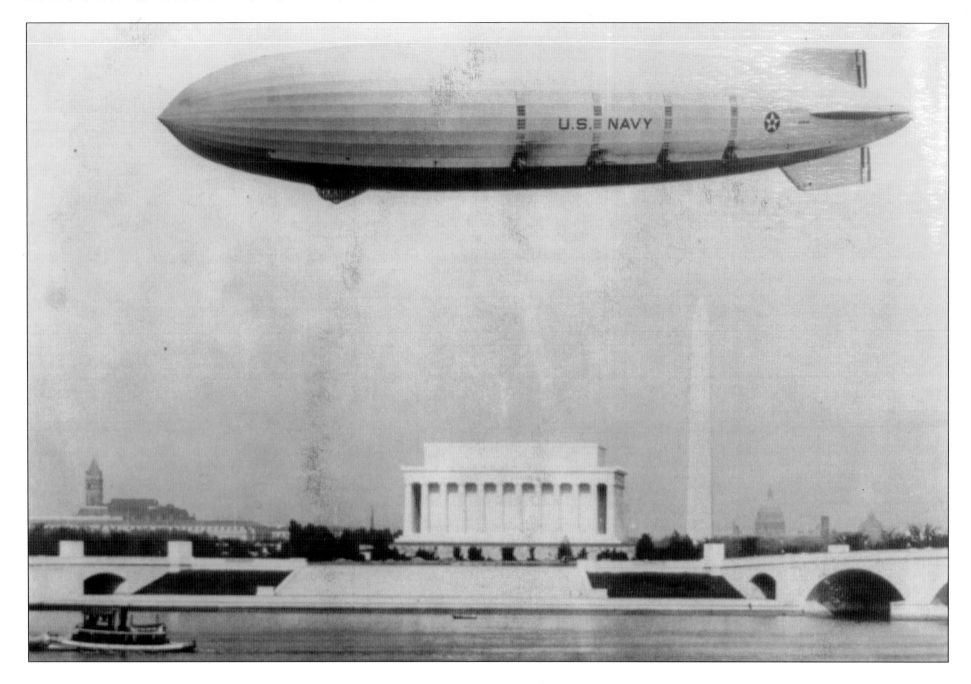

The airship *Akron* was one of the few American incursions into the short-lived aviation fad of rigid lighter-than-air aircraft. Built in its namesake Ohio city in 1931 along with its 1933 sister ship the *Macon*, it was still flying in this 1933 shot despite major changes in aircraft strategy underway at the time. The *Akron* would be lost at sea on April 4, 1933, with the loss of 70 lives, after less than 1,700 hours of flight over 20 months. Despite the use of nonflammable helium by U.S. airships, dirigibles fell out of favor after the fatal crashes of the *Shenandoah* in 1925 and the *Macon* in 1935 and the burning of the German *Hindenburg* in 1937.

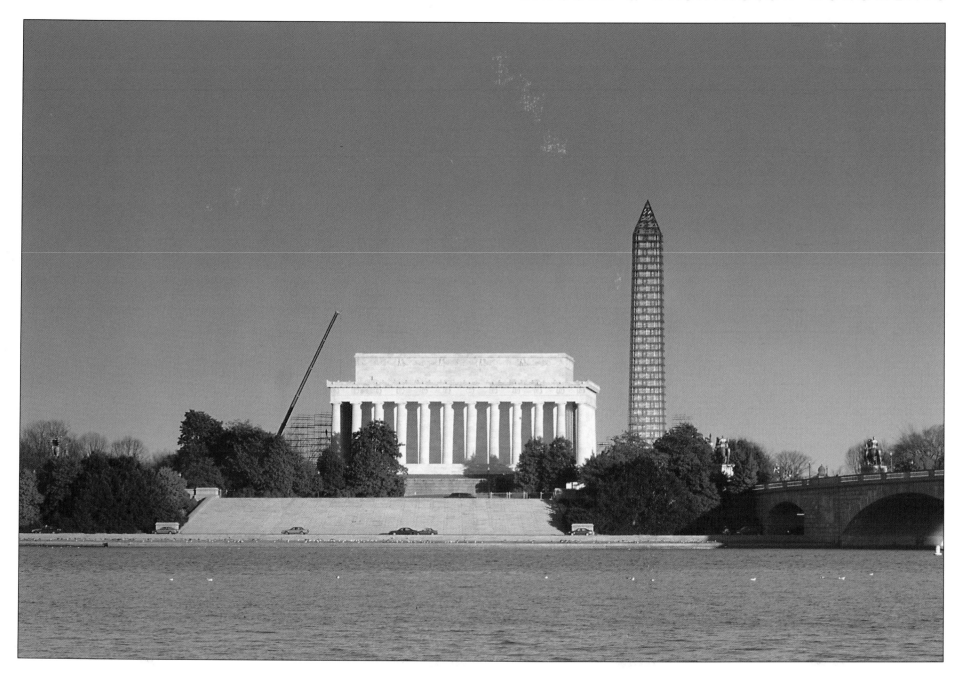

To the right of the modern photograph of the same view can be seen the east end of the Arlington Memorial Bridge, completed in 1932 to link Washington directly with Arlington National Cemetery. Beyond the Washington Monument (encased in Michael Graves' scaffolding during its restoration) and Lincoln Memorial in the distance can be seen the Old Post Office Tower. Today, jet aircraft swoop low over the location routinely on their approaches to Reagan National Airport (formerly Washington National Airport) to the south of the Pentagon in Arlington.

INDEX